Recovery, Meaning-Making, and Severe Mental Illness

Recovery, Meaning-Making, and Severe Mental Illness offers practitioners an integrative treatment model that will stimulate and harness their creativity, allowing for the formation of new ideas about wellness in the face of profound suffering. The model, Metacognitive Reflection and Insight Therapy (MERIT), complements current treatment modalities and can be used by practitioners from a broad range of theoretical backgrounds. By using metacognitive capacity as a guide to intervention, MERIT stretches and strengthens practitioners' capacity for reflection and allows them to better use their unique knowledge to help people who are confronting the suffering and chaos that often comes from psychosis. Clinicians will come away from this book with a variety of tools for helping clients manage their own recovery and confront the issues that accompany an illness-based identity.

Paul H. Lysaker, PhD, is a clinical psychologist and professor of clinical psychology in the Department of Psychiatry at the Indiana University School of Medicine. He has studied and provided psychotherapy to adults with serious mental illness for over 30 years. Dr. Lysaker is an author of over 400 peer-reviewed articles and is a member of the editorial boards of multiple professional journals.

Reid E. Klion, PhD, is a clinical psychologist and the chief operating officer of the MERIT Institute. His previous positions include assistant professor of psychiatry at the Indiana University School of Medicine and chief science officer at Performance Assessment Network, Inc. Dr. Klion has done work in areas ranging from psychotherapy to industrial-organizational psychology and test publishing.

Recovery, Meaning-Making, and Severe Mental Illness

A Comprehensive Guide to Metacognitive Reflection and Insight Therapy

Paul H. Lysaker and Reid E. Klion

Routledge
Taylor & Francis Group
NEW YORK AND LONDON

First edition published 2018
by Routledge
711 Third Avenue, New York, NY 10017

and by Routledge
2 Park Square, Milton Park, Abingdon, Oxon, OX14 4RN

Routledge is an imprint of the Taylor & Francis Group, an informa business

Library of Congress Cataloging-in-Publication Data
Names: Lysaker, Paul H., author. | Klion, Reid E., author.
Title: Recovery, meaning-making, and severe mental illness : a comprehensive guide to metacognitive reflection and insight therapy / Paul H. Lysaker and Reid E. Klion.
Description: First edition. | New York : Routledge, 2017. | Includes bibliographical references.
Identifiers: LCCN 2017030545 | ISBN 9781138208384 (hardcover : alk. paper) | ISBN 9781138208407 (pbk. : alk. paper) | ISBN 9781315447001 (e-book)
Subjects: | MESH: Mental Disorders—therapy | Cognitive Therapy—methods | Metacognition | Psychotherapeutic Processes | Models, Psychological
Classification: LCC RC467 | NLM WM 425.5.C6 | DDC 616.89—dc23
LC record available at https://lccn.loc.gov/2017030545

ISBN: 978-1-138-20838-4 (hbk)
ISBN: 978-1-138-20840-7 (pbk)
ISBN: 978-1-315-44700-1 (ebk)

Typeset in Galliard
by Apex CoVantage, LLC

Contents

List of Tables vii
Preface ix
About the Authors xi

SECTION I
Theoretical, Empirical, and Clinical Framework of MERIT 1

1 Introduction 3

2 Metacognitive Impairment and Serious Mental Illness 9

3 Understanding the Process of Metacognition 17

4 Assessing Metacognition and Its Role in Severe Mental Illness 25

SECTION II
MERIT's Preconditions and Eight Core Elements 31

5 Preconditions for Implementing MERIT 33

6 Overview of MERIT's Elements and Element 1: The Agenda 43

7 Element 2: Insertion of the Therapist's Mind 53

8 Element 3: Eliciting the Narrative Episode 61

9 Element 4: Defining the Psychological Problem 69

10 Element 5: Reflecting on the Therapeutic Relationship 79

11 Element 6: Reflecting on Progress 85

12 The MERIT-IF and Assessment of Metacognition During Sessions 91

13 Element 7: Stimulating Self-Reflection (S) and Awareness of the Other (O) 105

14 Element 8: Stimulating Mastery (M) 121

SECTION III
Implementation, Clinical, and Technical Issues 129

15 Practical Treatment Considerations and Learning MERIT 131

16 Common Clinical Issues 141

17 MERIT: Past and Future 149

Appendix I: MERIT Intervention Framework (MERIT-IF) 157

Appendix II: The MERIT Therapist Adherence Scale (MERIT-TAS) 159

References 163

Index 173

Tables

4.1	MAS-A Scales and Anchors	26
5.1	Preconditions for MERIT	41
6.1	MERIT Elements	43
6.2	Potential Agendas Expressed by a Simple Utterance	46
6.3	MERIT-TAS Element 1 Scale	52
7.1	Interventions to Sustain Dialogue	59
7.2	MERIT-TAS Element 2 Scale	60
8.1	MERIT-TAS Element 3 Scale	67
9.1	MERIT-TAS Element 4 Scale	76
10.1	MERIT-TAS Element 5 Scale	83
11.1	MERIT-TAS Element 6 Scale	89
12.1	Self-Reflectivity (S) Scale	93
12.2	Understanding Others' Minds (O) Scale	94
12.3	Mastery (M) Scale	95
12.4	Decentration (D) Scale	96
13.1	Characteristic Outcomes and Interventions for Self-Reflection (S)	106
13.2	Characteristic Outcomes and Interventions for Awareness of Others (O)	114
13.3	MERIT-TAS Element 7	119
14.1	MERIT-TAS Element 8	127
17.1	MERIT Psychotherapy Case Studies	151

Preface

MERIT is an integrative system of psychotherapy for adults with serious mental illness. It was not created in isolation. Key initial contributions came from Giancarlo Dimaggio, Susanne Harder, Ilanit Hasson-Ohayon, Andrew Gumley, and Kelly Buck. Two others, Jay Hamm and Bethany Leonhardt, joined this dialogue shortly after, and the name of MERIT was developed by Steven de Jong, Rozanne van Donkersgoed, and G. H. M. Pijnenborg. Others from our Indianapolis study group have contributed significantly to the development of this method including *Jenifer Vohs*, Marina Kukla, Kyle Minor, Sally Wasmuth, Elizabeth Belanger, Lauren Luther, Alison James, Benjamin Buck, Kelsey Bonfils, and Ruthie Firmin. The list of contributors also includes clinical colleagues Christina Silas, Jackie Hillis, Alysia Siegel, Sunita George, Ashley Schnackenberg, Elizabeth Smith, and Rebecca Fogley. Core support in Indianapolis has also come from Amy Strausberger and Nicole Beattie. Other support, from both North America and internationally, has come from Hamish McLeod, Robert Schweitzer, Ondrej Pec, Cumhur Taş, Leonor Irarrazaval, Jens Jensen, Nicolai Ladegaard, Sune Bo Hansen, Raffaele Popolo, and Giampaolo Salvatore. Others have provided considerable forms of support and these include David Pfenninger, David Roe, Philip Yanos, Antonio Semerari, and Martin Brüne.

About the Authors

Paul H. Lysaker is a graduate of Kenyon College and holds a PhD in clinical psychology from Kent State University. He has been active as a provider of clinical services to adults with serious mental illness since 1985. He is an author of over 400 peer-reviewed articles. He serves on the editorial board of many prestigious journals in the allied fields of mental health and has been the recipient of federal research funding since 2001. He is currently president of the MERIT Institute (www.meritinstitute.org).

Reid E. Klion is a graduate of Hobart College and holds a PhD in clinical psychology from Miami University. His professional work includes multiple publications in areas ranging from constructivist approaches to psychotherapy to industrial-organizational psychology, test publishing, and the use of technology in assessment. He is currently chief operating officer of the MERIT Institute (www.meritinstitute.org).

Section I

Theoretical, Empirical, and Clinical Framework of MERIT

1 Introduction

The Challenge of Severe Mental Illness

Serious mental illnesses, such as schizophrenia and other forms of psychosis, lead to a dizzying array of psychosocial and biological challenges that affect not only individuals but their friends, families, and communities as well. Both empirical research and first person accounts suggest it is virtually inevitable that these persons will confront a range of biological, social, political, and economic challenges. Serious mental illness also often involves impairment in the cognitive capacity to attend to, organize, and readily recall material within the flow of moment-to-moment life experiences. There may also be unusual or anomalous sensory experiences or disturbing beliefs and interpretations of social interactions.

Exacerbating the situation, persons with serious mental illness are also faced with stigma and stereotyped ideas about these disorders. From the media to the facilities where they seek treatment, the message is often communicated that they are incompetent, dangerous, or have lives that are simply less important or interesting than others. Difficulties in earning an income or pursuing educational opportunities may also stand in the way of improving one's circumstances. This is often compounded by a history of trauma which may also include the trauma associated with the experience of psychosis itself and its after effects.

From an historical perspective, while severe mental illness has been recognized in various forms for millennia, our scientific understanding of it has changed significantly in the last two decades. Beliefs about these conditions that were once seen as incontrovertible facts have not been supported by careful research. Additionally, many of the metaphors used to describe mental illness are problematic. This is perhaps best epitomized by the popular concept of the "broken brain," which does have the benefit of countering the common contemporary societal belief that persons diagnosed with mental illness are morally corrupt or responsible for their own suffering (Andreasen, 1984). It also serves to highlight how many of the features of mental illness are a consequence of disturbances in brain function and that individuals with these conditions are not to blame for their struggles. However, metaphors like this tell us little more than that people need help and risk suggesting that persons with mental illness may be somehow personally damaged or tainted. Further, they tell us little about how a unique individual might recover.

One of the most important lines of research that has shaken previous beliefs about mental illness concerns the course and ultimate outcomes of these disorders. It was once firmly believed that the most reasonable hope for people with serious mental illness was that they could have a life in which they were "stable" and free from acutely disturbed behaviors, thoughts, and feelings. The underlying belief was that people with these conditions would struggle to recover and had little chance of attaining a meaningful and satisfactory quality of life. However, recent work has found these pessimistic assumptions to be inaccurate. Research based upon interviews with persons diagnosed with severe mental illness find that they can recover over time and do find an acceptable quality of life, being not only free from the domination of symptoms but leading lives where they are meaningfully connected to their families and communities (Leonhardt et al., in press; Silverstein & Bellack, 2008).

This growing recognition that recovery from severe mental illness is possible should be an empowering message. Unfortunately, it appears that the mental health field is woefully unprepared for the task of helping persons to actually accomplish this. In addition to pharmacotherapy, which is broadly accepted as being critical but insufficient in and of itself, the current treatment approaches for persons with severe mental illnesses are largely comprised of discrete skills-based interventions designed to address specific issues such as social skills deficits, low self-esteem, poor knowledge of nutrition, and denial of illness. While certainly helpful in the right circumstances, this ever widening list of atomistic procedures loses sight that recovery is a matter for the whole person. Further, there is likely significant value in understanding the challenges faced by persons with severe mental illness in a deeper and more comprehensive manner rather than is afforded by approaching it as a set of skills deficits. As one patient said after completing a social skills group, "Well, I guess that was OK, but I have no idea why I might want to compliment someone in the first place."

Another important line of research into recovery from mental illness is that surveys of researchers, clinicians, public policy specialists, and persons diagnosed with these disorders indicate that there is not a clear consensus about how recovery should be defined and understood (Torgalsboen & Rund, 2002). For instance, remission of symptoms may be most important for some while establishing a lasting romantic and sexually intimate attachment will be at the forefront for others. Stated differently, the goals of recovery can be seen to potentially encompass many aspects of a person's life ranging from freedom from symptoms, developing a sense of hopefulness, the attainment of work and love, and restoration of a sense of the wholeness of one's sense of being (Davidson et al., 2005; Substance Abuse and Mental Health Services Administration, 2005; Slade, 2009), all depending upon the individual. This broader understanding of recovery, then, includes both objective outcomes such as symptom remission and the attainment of psychosocial milestones as well as more subjective elements such as having an improved quality of life and regaining a coherent sense of oneself as a valuable person in the world. Viewing recovery in this way also highlights that persons with mental illness must be enabled to direct the course of their own recovery.

Such an orientation toward recovery places a new onus on clinical practice. Treatment approaches must address the fact that individuals need to be empowered to attain the goals they want for their own lives and not have them predefined or provided by others. This also requires therapists to move beyond tactics that merely assist people to gain a particular skill, solve a specific problem, or provide a generic form of support. Instead, it necessitates a model of treatment that helps patients to make sense of the biological, social, psychological, and sociopolitical challenges they are facing, identify ways to respond to them, clarify the goals that they are seeking, and ultimately find a way to a personally satisfying and meaningful life.

Metacognitive Reflection and Insight Therapy (MERIT)

Metacognitive Reflection and Insight Therapy (MERIT) is a model of individual psychotherapy that is designed to meet the needs of adults who are seeking to recover from severe mental illness. It is based upon the premise that helping persons with severe mental illnesses to develop more complex understandings of themselves and others will enable them to better manage their lives and achieve their personal goals and aspirations (Lysaker & Roe, 2016).

MERIT can be successfully learned and provided by licensed mental health professionals trained to provide psychotherapy including psychiatrists, psychologists, social workers, occupational therapists, case workers, advanced practice nurses, and counselors. MERIT can be used as a stand-alone treatment approach, but it is not necessarily a replacement for existing psychiatric and rehabilitation practices. As such, it has been successfully implemented in conjunction with other interventions including medication management, supported employment, group and family counseling, psychoeducation, and peer counseling.

MERIT is an integrative model that can be offered by professionals who work from a variety of differing theoretical backgrounds. It provides practitioners trained in cognitive, behavioral, psychodynamic, humanistic, existential, family systems, psychiatric rehabilitation, and other perspectives with specific methodologies they can incorporate into their clinical practice. While MERIT is an approach to psychotherapy that is supported by science, it is not prescriptive and does not use the type of lock-step methodologies embodied by most contemporary treatment models. In a world of increasingly prescribed practice that focuses on isolated symptoms, specific problems, and a growing array of deficits, MERIT is concerned with the whole person. For practitioners who may feel stifled by the current treatment environment, it offers an approach that has the potential to stimulate and harness their creativity, allowing for the formation of new ideas about wellness in the face of some of the most profound suffering that confronts the mental health treatment community.

Focus on Metacognition

MERIT is concerned with meaning-making and the capacity for synthesizing information into a greater awareness of self and others. This is what forms our sense of personal identity and allows us to successfully deal with psychological and social challenges, and create a meaningful life for ourselves. MERIT uses the term "metacognition" to refer to the psychological processes that enable us to make sense of ourselves and the world. Metacognition is at play when we notice discrete things about ourselves and others and then synthesize that information into more complex and nuanced understandings. It is a mental process that is critical to the psychological health of all human beings. Awareness of our own and others' emotions, for example, enables us to determine how we might best respond when facing changing circumstances and situations. The capacity to appreciate what others may feel, their motivations, and how they may differ from us as individuals allows for relationships to endure and evolve when change or conflict emerge. Our metacognitive activities also allow us to make sense of our own unique joys and pains, the obstacles we encounter, and chart a path through life despite the adversities we face.

MERIT recognizes that the capacity for metacognition varies between persons. This means that individuals may be more or less able to discern what is happening within their own minds and in the minds of others. As a result, people can have a more or less fragmented sense of themselves, others, and the world. MERIT also recognizes that the many barriers to recovery noted earlier (e.g., stigma, neurocognitive compromise, symptoms, trauma, and poverty) can compromise a person's metacognitive capacity, ultimately interfering with the ability to direct his or her own recovery. As a result, individuals whose metacognitive capacities are diminished will have difficulties in understanding and effectively responding to the problems they face. To this point, MERIT views impairments in metacognition as a key underlying factor in severe mental illness.

Structured Interventions Oriented to Recovery

MERIT seeks to promote recovery by assisting people to improve their metacognitive capacities and does so through using interventions that are tailored and targeted to the patient's current level of functioning. By helping to improve metacognitive capacity, MERIT facilitates collaborative exploration with patients about their lives, developing a sense of what has been lost, what is hoped for, and what to seek in the future. MERIT is rather unique in its use of a validated method for assessing metacognitive capacity in the course of a psychotherapy session which allows treatment to be effectively adapted for persons regardless of the severity of their symptoms. Rather than using a prescriptive curriculum, lesson plan, or instructions for what content should be introduced and discussed in sessions, the practice of MERIT is defined by a set of eight measurable processes and therapist activities, called elements, that should occur in every psychotherapy session.

Overview of Book

This book will describe and discuss how to use MERIT in clinical practice. It is divided into three sections. In the first section, Chapters 2 and 3 discuss the concept of metacognition and its role in treating persons with severe mental illnesses. Chapter 4 explores the measurement of metacognition. The second section, Chapters 5 through 14, represents the core of the book and describes assumptions that underlie MERIT and the eight key elements that define its practice. The final section, Chapters 15 through 17, discusses how MERIT begins, its treatment phases, common clinical and technical dilemmas, and future directions.

A Note on Terminology

Before beginning, a few words are needed regarding the basic terms that will be used in this book. First, we use the word "patient" to describe a person receiving this form of psychotherapy. We realize this is a controversial term that may offend some. Certainly, many people who have received mental health care have felt stigmatized and marginalized by those experiences. Others also believe that the word "patient" positions the sufferer in a passive stance and does not capture the idea that wellness requires an active role in the face of suffering. As a result, terms such as service users, clients, consumers, and even psychiatric survivors have been used to replace patient. We chose to use "patient" given its roots in both the Latin and Greek words meaning "to suffer," recognizing that people with these conditions do indeed suffer. We eschew any implication that this term places a person in a passive role because it is diametrically opposed to what MERIT hopes to achieve but acknowledge that others may prefer a different term.

Much of the research foundation for MERIT is based upon work with persons with schizophrenia. This term is also not without controversy. Many suggest this term is stigmatizing and question whether there is a sufficient scientific basis for claiming that there are a distinct group of disorders that could be called schizophrenia spectrum disorders. In Europe, in fact, the term is being replaced with the term psychosis. As a result, we use this word (as well as the term "severe mental illness") with caution but also acknowledge its controversial use. We are more comfortable with this term than others, again given its roots in ancient Greek for the splitting or shattering of the mind, which we see as an apt explanation for the fragmentation of associations that often occurs in those with schizophrenia.

Finally, we consider MERIT to be a form of psychotherapy. While the term "psychotherapy" itself is not a very controversial one, there is a history of psychotherapy as being seen as harmful to persons with serious mental illness and their families. A little more than a half century ago, several psychotherapists suggested that psychotherapy could cure psychosis by treating the destructive effects of maladaptive family communication (Karon & Vandenbos, 1977). On the other hand, some have expressed the concern that a psychotherapeutic relationship may represent another parental relationship in which the mentally person is again marginalized (Mueser & Berenbaum, 1990). That being said, we hope to show how a consultative and respectful relationship that focuses on metacognition can empower persons to reject stigma, abandon the sick role, develop hope, determine how they want to manage the mental health challenges that they face, and find a fulfilling life for themselves.

As a final stylistic note, we interchangeably use gendered single person pronouns such as him/her and his/hers to refer to patients and therapists throughout this work.

2 Metacognitive Impairment and Serious Mental Illness

How Does Serious Mental Illness Interrupt a Life?

Serious mental illnesses such as schizophrenia and other forms of psychosis profoundly interrupt the lives of millions of people worldwide. Persons who once dreamed of fulfilling social roles such as teachers or doctors, parents, husbands or wives, as well as others who once fulfilled those roles but lost them, find themselves without firm goals or even a sense of what has happened to change the course of their lives. They and those around them can see that the trajectory of their lives has been altered, if not shattered, but cannot find a clear explanation for why this has happened. Why did a life that was moving forward stop and sometimes even seem to have gone away completely? Simply offering the label of schizophrenia as a cause is not an adequate explanation nor is it particularly helpful in assisting persons with these disorders.

MERIT is based upon the belief that the collapse of the ability to form complex and integrated ideas about the self and others is strongly linked with the major disruptions in life course that are often seen in persons with severe mental illness. Metacognitive capacity is critical for persons with severe mental illnesses because it is central to making sense of and responding to biological, social, psychological, and economic challenges posed by their conditions. MERIT does not hold that these deficits necessarily cause or result in psychosis, but that they severely hinder the ability to make sense of, cope with, and recover from these conditions.

This view is notably at odds with many other perspectives. According to many in the field, serious mental illness is at best treated as a collection of skill deficits, a form of distorted self-experience, or multiple discrete symptoms that often involve odd ideas or experiences. From the perspective of MERIT, the model that the lives of persons with serious mental illness are interrupted largely due to the loss of skills is unsatisfying and incomplete. First person accounts, research, and clinical reports detail how serious mental illnesses typically do not begin as a matter of not knowing how to perform particular acts or discrete skills. Rather, mental illness often begins at the subjective level in the form of explicit disturbances in sense of self or in how persons experience who they are as a being in the world (Andresen et al., 2003; Dimaggio et al., 2009).

People with serious mental illness explain that they feel they have lost part of themselves or cannot make sense of how they are connected to others (Buck et al., 2013; Kean, 2009; Lampshire, 2012; Lauveng, 2012; Roe & Ben-Yishai, 1999, Roe & Davidson, 2005). Similarly, views of serious mental illness as primarily odd or unusual self-experience (Parnas & Handest, 2003) also do not fully explain the phenomenon. It is established that many with mental illness can poignantly describe their suffering in ways that we can all relate to. The "self" of a person with schizophrenia is not odd, different, or deformed, but is a self in profound pain as it interacts with the world (Hamm et al., 2015; Searles, 1965; Sullivan, 1962). Finally, views of serious mental illness as higher levels in the natural continuum of odd or suspicious thinking are unsatisfying as many people can have very odd views, thrive in a range of settings, and sometimes attain notable positions in our political and social systems.

All human beings decide how to pursue their lives, including work and relationships, on the basis of the meanings they have assigned to themselves and the world. For example, a person's decision to leave a job or a relationship is based upon the perceived meaning she attributes to it or perhaps the anticipated outcome. Consider a graduate student who considered leaving her program after being severely criticized by her previously supportive faculty advisor and feeling unsure, betrayed, and ashamed after failing several important exams. This student would be more likely to persist if attaining that degree held deep personal meaning for her. Conversely, another person might be more willing to consider leaving if the degree had come to mean little to her or if she could see different, more promising options for her future that had nothing to do with completing the program.

Impairment in Meaning-Making and the Experience of Fragmentation in Schizophrenia: A Brief History

MERIT views disruptions in the meaning-making process, or the ability to form complex and integrated ideas about the self and others that we use to guide our lives, as a parsimonious explanation for the collapse in a life often seen in schizophrenia. The belief that impairments in conceptual thinking are a key feature of severe mental illness is not new or unique to MERIT. Indeed, it is consistent with what Eugen Bleuler, the Swiss psychiatrist who coined the term "schizophrenia," observed in his seminal work *Dementia Praecox, or the Group of Schizophrenia*. In this work, originally published in 1911 and first translated into English in 1950, Bleuler, in collaboration with his colleague Carl Jung, described prolonged psychosis as a comprehensible human phenomenon. He distanced himself from the idea that it was a progressive dementia and described the psychological forces he believed directly disrupted functioning.

Bleuler (1950) described the group of adults in an asylum whose lives had been profoundly interrupted. Like patients suffering with dementia, the course of their lives seemed to have been completely altered. They had inexplicably stopped forming and pursuing basic life goals. These patients, however, did not have the kinds of gross cognitive deficits found in persons with dementia who often cannot carry out the basics of daily life without supervision or even accurately recall the basic details of their lives. This was not the case in what Bleuler called schizophrenia, where patients knew who they were and could often carry out a daily routine yet seemed to be in a fog and interpersonally distant.

In trying to understand this, Bleuler suggested that these patients experienced a range of deficits (which were later referred to as Bleuler's "Four As" (Bleuler, 1950)). The first and primary of these involved "association" (Bleuler's First "A"), which was the loss of the ability to link ideas together with associative threads. Here, Bleuler appears to have explicitly connected the ability to make sense of the world with the capacity to behave in an adaptive fashion. Because patients could not see how different ideas might be related to one another or how the ideas they formed contained irrelevant or discordant elements, their thinking was often unhelpful for directing purposeful activity. Bleuler (1950) wrote, "It appears as if the pathways of association and inhibition, established by experience, had lost their meaning and significance" (p. 350). The result was that "the patient hardly knows how to orient himself either inwardly or outwardly . . . a very intelligent patient needs hours of strenuous inner effort to find her own ego for a few brief moments" (p. 143).

Carl Jung made a similar observation in his earlier work in 1906, *On the Psychology of Dementia Praecox*, later translated in 1944. Citing the disruption of associative processes as evident in word association tests, Jung did not claim that these were only his and Bleuler's ideas but gave credit to earlier work which used terms like "apperceptive dementia," suggesting that the condition was seen to involve deficits in the ability to think about mental states in complex ways since the earliest days of the field.

There were others who also linked psychosis with impairments in the ability to integrate information into a complex sense of self and others. Emil Kraepelin, who coined the earlier term of "dementia praecox," wrote, "Dementia praecox is a series of states the common characteristic of which is a peculiar destruction of the internal connection of the psychic personality. . . . The effects of the injury predominate the emotional and volitional spheres of life" (1919, p. 3). While Kraepelin presented a substantially different view than Bleuler, he also described how persons with schizophrenia had lost a sense of personal meaning, which impaired their ability to direct their own lives due to a lack of coherent connections between different aspects of self-experience. In this work, he suggests that the core connection that integrates the psychology of a person had been lost.

At roughly the same time, Freud described psychosis as involving difficulties in synthesizing ideas, which led to the loss of the capacity to synthesize experience into a complex and useful sense of self. Freud believed that in psychosis "instead of binding images, affects and ideas into a coherent whole that characterizes the secondary process, a process of unbinding takes over and dominates the apperception of the world in the states of psychosis . . . altogether, the unbinding causes a breach in the unity and identity of the self and threatens the many symbolic links characterizing its integrating capacities and its reality testing" (Rosenbaum, 2005, p. 83).

Unfortunately, interest in this striking early confluence of work suggesting a model that schizophrenia and other psychotic disorders were the result of conceptual fragmentation has diminished over the years though it has not vanished entirely. As an example, Andreasen and colleagues (1998), summarizing neural imaging research, proposed that schizophrenia is the result of a compromise in the neural circuitry that allows basic brain structures to work together and integrate information. They write that this disruption "produces 'cognitive dysmetria,' difficulty in prioritizing, processing, coordinating, and responding to information. This poor mental coordination is a fundamental cognitive deficit in schizophrenia and can account for its broad diversity of symptoms" (p. 203). While Andreasen et al. (1998) were not explicitly concerned with self-experience, they did suggest that schizophrenia fundamentally interferes with how ideas about the world are formed within the flow of daily life. Making a similar argument about work on electrophysiology, Vlcek et al. (2014) suggest that "deficits in the integrity of connections between various brain areas . . . produces disconnection of information, disrupted binding, and disintegration of consciousness that in terms of modern neuroscience could connect original Bleuler's concept of 'split mind' with research of neural information integration" (p. 1309).

This residual ongoing interest in the role of conceptual fragmentation aside, the focus of most contemporary work on the psychopathology of schizophrenia has been concerned with specific disruptions in function that are studied in isolation. Whether at the level of the molecule, brain region, or behavior, this work describes discrete impairments or abnormalities that only offer a rather isolated picture of human experience. As we have suggested elsewhere, this hyper-specific focus reflects "a trend in which we are offered precise accounts of the pieces of schizophrenia that, without an overarching picture of the disorder, exist functionally as fragments" (Nemeroff et al., 2013, p. 202).

Challenges in Assessing Metacognition

One significant factor that has impeded inquiry into the role of conceptual integration in severe mental illness is that there has not been a good way to systematically measure a person's capacity to form complex mental representations. This task is much more demanding and nuanced than simply determining whether a specific response is correct or not. Rather, integration needs to be understood in terms of its complexity and adaptiveness for each unique individual.

Suppose you were asked to find five people who know you well. Each would have a reasonable sense of who you are and would likely be able to identify something unique about you. Their descriptions would very likely vary from each other because each has integrated information about you in a different matter; as a result, there is no single "right" idea about who you are. Nevertheless, you can distinguish people who understand you well from those who do not. In contrast, consider another set of people who are only casual acquaintances. While they have interacted with you long enough to know you in general terms, they are unlikely to have a very nuanced understanding of who you are. While both sets of people have an understanding of you, your close friends are able to describe you in a more integrated and complex fashion.

The same is true about the ideas we hold about ourselves. It is very likely that how we see ourselves as a unique being at this very moment in our lives is different than how we understood ourselves ten years ago. Much has happened across that span of time that has been integrated into our sense of who we are, hopefully leading to a deeper sense of ourselves. This integration allows us to experience an identity that is both continuous and evolving with time.

The process of integration is paradoxical in the sense that it is often unimaginably complex but also something we often engage in automatically with little conscious effort as we go about our lives. For example, consider meeting someone for the first time at a social gathering. At the conclusion of the evening during which you spent some time with her, you will have some initial holistic idea of that person. Much more than causal speculation, your sense of her will embody crucial ideas about how you expect she is likely to act, whether you are able to like or trust her, whether she has a sense of humor, how she is similar to other people you know, and a whole variety of other factors. Forming this concept requires the integration of many pieces of information. Just to name a few, these would include her appearance, age, ethnicity, and gender. Your idea of her might also include the cadence of her speech, whether her language was formal or casual, the words she used, her facial expressions, as well as how she interacted with others and how they responded. You might reflect on how she reminds you of other people in your life. There might also be an awareness of your own somatic and subjective responses when you interacted with her. For example, did you feel relaxed or tense? You also might incorporate information that you may have learned about her previously or how you might expect her to act if you were to meet again.

This integrative process allows us to pull all this information together into a gestalt where the whole is not reducible to the sum of its parts. Knowing another person is a matter of organizing information about her into an overarching conceptual structure, and it is less important whether we can recall every detail. A large part of this takes place in an instantaneous and preconscious process where certain details are deemed irrelevant and not significantly influencing the understanding of the larger whole of the person.

A similar process can be found in how people form a larger sense and understanding of themselves. Here, consider what you might think if you had had a conflict with the person you met at the social event. Thinking about yourself in this context, there is a vast array of information that could be potentially integrated into your vision of yourself. You felt a certain way during the argument, with other complicated emotions potentially arising in you during and after the conflict. You made certain familiar comments and may have realized this person reminds you of others who have elicited similar reactions in you. You also remember the last time you behaved this way. You may also imagine how other people you know might have thought about the conflict and what they might have thought about you. You wonder what the person with whom you had the conflict is thinking about you as well as the events and emotions that led up to it. You might also notice how your ideas of the other person have changed or wonder if you are thinking clearly about it. And with whatever larger sense of yourself that emerges, you may need to integrate and make sense of this as well.

Integration, Behavior, and Mental Illness

It is critical to realize that the ideas that you form about another person are not idle speculations. Rather, they will guide you and become the basis for how you will act with her in the future, if and when and with what you can trust her, when she might be helpful and not helpful, even how you should read the social cues she offers. If a person is unable to form integrated ideas of others, he could well be doomed to live in a world that seems fragmented where there are only very vague or confusing rules for relating. There would be no basis for understanding others in nuanced ways or forming enduring and meaningful connections with others.

The integrative process is essential and forms the basis for choosing what to do next and for learning from what just happened. It informs whether you want to ignore this person in the future, seek reconciliation, or perhaps pursue the opportunity for another confrontation. The ideas you form about this interaction can also help you to understand the distress you may be experiencing about it in the moment and how to manage it. Additionally, these ideas may also allow you to see how others may have understood the situation and how they might have responded differently from you.

Looking back at the work of psychiatry's early pioneers, if they were correct in describing how impairments in the process of meaning-making are a primary feature of severe mental illness, this provides a powerful lens to understand the subjective experience of persons with these disorders. If someone were unable to appreciate not only how all the different elements are at play in both themselves and others, but also lacked the capacity to synthesize them into effective understandings of their world, that world would become a profoundly confusing place because there would be no way to understand one's own experience or to utilize connections with others to think about it. If these difficulties with making sense of what is happening in one's own mind are combined with difficulties making sense of what is happening in the minds of others, one might readily understand how this might profoundly interrupt a person's life.

3 Understanding the Process of Metacognition

MERIT's View of Metacognition

MERIT uses the term "metacognition" to describe the processes at work when people integrate experiences and form complex ideas about themselves and others. In the strictest sense, metacognition is a thought about a thought, but it is generally used in a broader sense to refer to a mental act in which a person forms a thought or idea about his own or the other's mental activities. The construct came to be broadly used over 35 years ago in education research (e.g., Flavell, 1979) and was quickly adopted by a multitude of other fields and research paradigms, including cognitive psychology to capture awareness of memories and the feeling of knowing something (Bacon et al., 2001; Thompson et al., 2011), and in psychopathology to describe the specific things people tend to think about (Bennett & Wells, 2010; Wells, 2000), the ability to monitor errors and correct behavior (Koren et al., 2004), and the capacity to monitor one's own process of reasoning (Moritz et al., 2007). Additionally, attachment researchers have used the term to describe the emergence of self-awareness and awareness of others within infant caretaker dyads (Main, 1991). However, as Tarricone (2011) observed, one of the problems with widespread interest in metacognition is that "its many facets and rich conceptual history" have created a "fuzziness" and "obscurity surrounding the construct" (p. 3). This is exacerbated by the fact that it has been used to describe a number of phenomena that may only be rather distantly related to each other.

MERIT's use of this concept is based on Antonio Semerari and colleagues' (2003) and Giancarlo Dimaggio and colleagues' (2007, 2013, 2012, 2015) description of metacognition as a larger process in which information is integrated into representations of the self and others in ways that will vary in their complexity. Their perspective stresses the representational nature of thinking and that our ideas about ourselves and others are a construction rather than a mirror of reality. Seeing metacognition as a matter of integration rather than capturing a pure and correct perception echoes Dewey (1922) who remarked that people know themselves and others as "an integration" of multiple facets and not simply the sum of a collection of data. The discrete processes of metacognition such as error detection and emotion recognition are needed to form complex ideas about the self and others; however, it takes synthetic processes to bring together a range of different aspects to form complex representations which can grow in coherence and complexity over time and flexibly change as called for in new experiences.

MERIT conceptualizes metacognition as encompassing a broad spectrum of mental activities (Lysaker, Bob et al., 2013; Lysaker, Vohs et al., 2013). At one end of the spectrum is the awareness of discrete and highly specific mental experiences such as thoughts, emotions, or wishes. Examples of this might include an awareness that you are anxious, wanting or desiring a certain thing, or ruminating about something. At the other end are the larger thoughts that are the product of the integration of those discrete experiences. This might be realizing you are anxious because you have a feeling of a lack of control over the circumstances which now surround you or that you are ruminating due to feeling devalued in a recent interaction which was similar to a number of childhood experiences. We need activities from both sides of the metacognitive spectrum in order to make sense of our daily experience. The ideas we form of ourselves are based on an awareness of discrete elements of experience, and the sense we make of our discrete experiences is constructed from how we understand ourselves in that context. One is necessary for the other and each affects the other. For instance, awareness that a wish or thought does not fit into your larger picture of yourself would necessitate either an alteration in your interpretation of that experience, how you understand yourself, or both.

MERIT's Assumptions About Metacognition

Metacognition Has Multiple Foci

Synthesizing literature from the disciplines of developmental psychology, attachment theory, cognitive psychology, and psychotherapy, Semerari and Dimaggio suggest that metacognition involves four different kinds of acts (Semerari et al., 2003). They are reflections about the self (self-reflectivity), reflection upon the experiences of other people (awareness of the mind of the other), awareness that events can be understood validly from multiple perspectives (decentration), and reflections about how awareness of the self and others can be used to respond to emergent psychological and social challenges (mastery).

A key point that Semerari and Dimaggio make is that there is not necessarily a high degree of correlation between these metacognitive capacities. For instance, having complex thoughts about oneself can make it easier to have complex thoughts about others, but it is possible that some persons may have better abilities to reflect upon themselves as opposed to reflecting about others, or vice versa. Similarly, some people may have relatively intact abilities to think about themselves or others but be unable to respond effectively to emotional distress based on that information. As will be detailed in later chapters, these insights are foundational for MERIT because they lead to the conclusion that any therapy focused on improving an individual's metacognition needs to specifically target each of these metacognitive functions.

Metacognition Is Essential for Survival

A second point is that metacognition is not an erudite activity which people perform only when all other basic needs are met or a late night activity which only the privileged engage in once the more important work of the day is done. On the contrary, making sense of the world around us is necessary for survival and takes place on an ongoing and continual basis every day. The ideas we form and our ability to reflect upon and use those ideas are essential for survival. Indeed, our metacognitive activities form the basis for what we decide to pursue, how, and with whom. Harkening back to existential psychiatry, human beings pursue certain ends not only because they know how to but also because they know why they should (Frankl, 1965). In this way, metacognitive processes provide the "why" which impels us to find a "how."

It is also through this process that we make sense of and live with distress without it necessarily derailing our lives. Following Nietzsche's dictum, metacognitive abilities allow us to make sense of fear and anger and decide when they are warranted. These abilities help us know when we should respond to a sense of being ill at ease by protecting ourselves and alternately when we are pointlessly harboring ill will against others who might contribute positively to our lives. When our metacognitive processes fail, we trust the wrong people, miss opportunities, and risk a profound sense of confusion, alienation, and isolation. Framed in this way, the lens of metacognition allows us to see the struggle of persons with serious mental illness as being firmly within the realm of recognizable and understandable human experience.

Metacognition Is a Fundamentally Intersubjective Act

MERIT holds that human beings make sense of their own mental states and those of others in either an actual or an imagined dialogue. This is essential because it allows us to see that human beings can only make meaning in ways that can be shared and acknowledged between people. Our understandings of self and others, both complex and simple, are formed in the context of real or imagined interactions with others, not in a radically isolated mind. None of us can decide on our own who we are as unique human beings. For example, none of us really has the privilege to decide independently that we are funny, empathic, or not self-centered. Indeed, experience suggests that people who think they are funny, empathic, or not self-centered when others do not share that opinion are subject to friendly ridicule at best.

Metacognition, simply put, occurs and evolves intersubjectively. The term "intersubjectivity" refers to what is occurring between two minds (Beebe et al., 2005). Like metacognition, it can also refer to a spectrum of activities.

More narrow definitions stress how intersubjectivity describes the experience of shared states of mind while broader definitions use the term to pinpoint the mutual understanding of the other's subjective experience (Stern, 2000). Intersubjectivity is a type of communication unique to humans, at least in its more developed forms, and is regarded as a precondition for the development of self-reflection and the emergence of the narratization of experience in very young children (Cortina & Liotti, 2010).

From a clinical perspective, the recognition that integration is intersubjective is critical because patients make sense of their experiences and challenges and ultimately move toward recovery alongside and with therapists. MERIT therapists do not make meaning for patients nor do they correct, steer, or "get" patients to think certain things. Further, by understanding metacognition as an intersubjective act, MERIT does not see the process by which persons form a sense of themselves and others as a simple hypercognitive act. Rather, metacognition goes well beyond an isolated mind and involves the integration of bodily experiences, complex thought, and the experiences and perspectives of others.

Metacognition Is a Capacity

Not only does MERIT share Semerari and Dimaggio's view that there may be variability between an individual's metacognitive abilities but it also asserts that these will vary from person to person. For instance, some may be better able to integrate information and form complex ideas about themselves and others or more able to see situations from multiple perspectives than others. Additionally, some situations pose more challenges to metacognitive capacity than others. It is easier to think about oneself in a calm, supportive environment than in a situation filled with anger and frustration or when facing someone else in a hostile state. There are also certain things that are more difficult to integrate than others. For example, making sense of why you were kind to a stranger might be far easier to understand than why you behaved in a selfish way toward a long-standing friend. Nevertheless, MERIT thinks about metacognitive capacities in a manner loosely analogous to blood pressure. Blood pressure is a relatively stable phenomenon which nevertheless can change in stressful situations (e.g., during a conflict in the absence of support or in circumstances that feel threatening). In a similar manner, it is assumed a general assessment can be made of metacognitive capacity with the understanding it may or may not change in situations that vary in terms of emotional intensity, personal motivation, context, and the availability of social support.

These assumptions are not academic. The clinical implication of central importance is that metacognition can grow or diminish as a capacity. One of MERIT's fundamental beliefs is that the metacognitive capacities of persons with serious mental illness can be improved. This is to say that with treatment or with other favorable conditions, persons can become more able to integrate information. Thus, as will be echoed throughout this guidebook, enhanced metacognitive capacity is the key outcome of treatment. Moreover, the elements of MERIT, which will be presented in several chapters, have been designed to provide the maximal support for the emergence of higher levels of metacognitive capacity.

Deficits in Metacognition May Result From Multiple Factors

Deficits in metacognition can be caused in multiple and often overlapping ways. They may reflect a failure for the person to have ever developed these capacities due to interpersonal trauma such as abuse, neglect, or the failure to form secure attachments. For example, someone may never have had the kind of relationships with caretakers or peers that offered a forum for developing the ability to bring together information about oneself and others. Alternatively, those deficits may reflect a deterioration of previous capacities. For instance, metacognitive capacity can atrophy if not utilized in dialogue with others as may occur with people who have been isolated, marginalized, or stigmatized, and as a result have few opportunities to think about themselves and their lives. Trauma, which may play a role in the development of psychosis, or the trauma of the experience of psychosis, may also lead to reductions in metacognitive capacity. In such situations, the traumatic event itself may pose information which is difficult to integrate or may make it threatening to place oneself in a vulnerable reflective position with others, especially when the trauma is interpersonal.

Impairments in neurocognitive function, which are common in persons with severe mental illness, may also compromise metacognitive capacity. Difficulties with memory, for example, may make it difficult to link current experiences to the past and lead to challenges in seeing how one's mental states have changed over time. Attentional deficits may impair the ability to determine what elements in a given situation should be afforded more salience than others, making it hard to distinguish the relevant from the irrelevant. Deficits in executive function and abstract thinking may also make it difficult to shift between different perspectives, interfering with the process of integrating pertinent information into larger representations. Regardless of the specific etiological factors which may have contributed to an individual's metacognitive deficits, MERIT utilizes the same treatment approach to support the emergence of higher levels of metacognitive capacity.

Other Concepts Related to Metacognition

While MERIT's notion of metacognition is conceptually similar to a number of other constructs including social cognition, mentalization, mindfulness, emotional intelligence, and healthy ego function, it differs from them in some significant ways as well. For example, *social cognition* refers to a range of different cognitive, affective, automatic, and willful processes that enable people to form ideas about social exchanges and includes theory of mind, affect recognition, and attributional style (Brüne et al., 2011). While metacognition has been described as a component of social cognition (Pinkham et al., 2014), one important difference is that social cognition is expressly interested in the *correct detection* of a discrete thought or feeling. In contrast, MERIT is concerned with how metacognitive activity serves to integrate details into a whole coherence, not absolute correctness. Metacognition is also concerned with the ability to shift back and forth from one's own perspective to that of others and sees meaning-making as a process that takes place within discourse and doubts the meaningfulness or accuracy of separate perceptions when considered in isolation. This is similar to what the fictional detective Nero Wolfe expressed when he chided his assistant in the novel *Fer-de-Lance* for not seeing the larger picture: "As usual you are so engrossed in the fact that you are oblivious to its environment" (Stout, 1983, p. 284). Said another way, metacognition does not deny that we can "get it wrong" or "get it right" when interacting with others but is more concerned with what surrounds and leads to our ideas of what has happened and what is to be done about it.

Mentalization, a concept used by a prominent school of psychoanalysis that is deeply concerned with genuine versus less genuine forms of integrated self-reflection (Fonagy et al., 2004), may overlap with metacognition more closely than social cognition. However, metacognition explicitly distinguishes awareness of self and other from the ability to use that metacognitive capacity. This allows MERIT to understand how persons can form complex ideas about themselves and others but still be unable to use that information effectively in response to psychological challenges, as may be a prominent problem in borderline personality disorder as opposed to psychosis (Semerari et al., 2014). Additionally, metacognition rejects mentalization's perspective that deficits in reflectivity occur almost exclusively in the context of disturbed attachment. MERIT, by contrast, understands attachment security as potentially separate from metacognitive capacity (Outcalt et al., 2016) because the integrative processes used in relationships may be either more or less dysfunctional outside the interpersonal context. As a result, unlike mentalization, MERIT does not conceptualize emotional regulation as a precondition for metacognitive activity but sees them as mutually influential processes so that enhancing metacognition may lead to better emotion regulation and vice versa.

Like metacognition, *mindfulness* and *emotional intelligence* are both concerned with increasing self-awareness and insight into the emotional states of others. However, like social cognition and theory of mind, neither of these constructs are explicitly concerned with how these forms of awareness are integrated and assembled into higher order structures. Both seem to assume this integration will be a natural consequence of awareness whereas MERIT's concept of metacognition allows integration to be seen as an incremental process that can be studied and the subject of direct intervention.

MERIT's view of integration may have most in common with psychoanalytic explorations of *ego function* in schizophrenia. In particular, Bellack (1971) has suggested a core feature of schizophrenia is the loss of *synthetic-integrative functioning* which "is the capacity of the organism to reconcile or integrate discrepancies in attitudes, values, affects, behaviors and self-representation" (p. 30). Like metacognition, this construct is concerned with how different elements of experience are integrated. However, MERIT holds that that integration occurs within discourse and is fundamentally intersubjective. In contrast, the concept of an ego function is a far more mentalistic task. For instance, the tasks that Bellack suggest tap this construct generally do not involve any form of social exchange but are based on perceptual organization and use stimuli that the participant either has to extrapolate from or ignore. Further, while MERIT distinguishes between different levels in integration and is intimately concerned with how that information is used, this psychoanalytic approach is largely concerned with increasing this conceptual capacity but with little attention paid to defining the stages of its development. Finally, deficits in this ego function model are closely linked with an inability to regulate basic drives and the lack of non-primitive defense mechanisms. By contrast, MERIT conceptualizes metacognitive capacity to be distinct from how persons protect themselves from the experience of unacceptable wishes and thoughts.

4 Assessing Metacognition and Its Role in Severe Mental Illness

In the last chapter, we detailed how MERIT conceptualizes metacognition. In this chapter, we turn now to how MERIT quantifies metacognition. The ability to assess metacognition is important because it allows us to test two of MERIT's basic assertions: (i) persons with serious mental illness have deficits in metacognition, and (ii) these deficits are associated with functional impairments. We will also review how these measures makes it possible to determine whether metacognition changes over time in response to treatment.

Prior efforts to measure disturbances in metacognition have proven to be less than satisfying. Assessments do exist which can capture how well an individual can accurately guess someone else's emotions or intentions based upon role plays, video clips, pictures, or cartoons. These tools are often used to demonstrate how persons with serious mental illness may misunderstand social exchanges. However, they fail to capture how different kinds of complex information are integrated into an evolving understanding of another person.

There are also several methods for assessing the ability to correctly recognize one's own mental states. In these paradigms, persons are given tasks or questionnaires that assess whether they can distinguish their own actions, emotions, and memories as well as if they are making errors in this process. However, they share the same limitations of the methods used for measuring the accurate detection of others' emotions because they are so distant from the real-life process of how we actually experience internal states in the moment and synthesize them into a meaningful sense of self.

Metacognition Assessment Scale-Abbreviated (MAS-A)

The need for an assessment that would be able to accurately capture of the complexity of metacognition led to the development of the Metacognition Assessment Scale-Abbreviated (MAS-A; Lysaker et al., 2005). Our work was inspired by Semarari et al.'s (2003) Metacognition Assessment Scale (MAS). The original MAS was based on an integration of research and theoretical work on attachment, cognition, psychopathology, and human development.

As a measure of how human beings think about themselves and others while engaged in the flow of daily life while reflecting about the past and future, it was used to assess changes in psychotherapy.

The MAS-A retains the MAS's four scale structure labeling the scales Self-Reflectivity (S), Understanding Others' Minds (O), Decentration (D), and Mastery (M). In a crucial change, the MAS-A was transformed into a dimensional tool where each scale rated metacognitive functioning on a dimension ranging from highly fragmented to highly integrated. This allows a rater to assess a person's maximal capacity and assign a single value to each of the four MAS-A scales (see Table 4.1).

The MAS-A assesses a person's metacognitive capacity by determining the highest level of metacognitive activity that is evident in a subject's narrative using a research interview known as the Indiana Psychiatric Illness Interview (IPII; Lysaker et al., 2002). Since the MAS-A scales are conceptualized as involving increasingly complex and less fragmented activities, it is assumed that once an activity or scale item is found to be beyond the capacity of the participant, no other scale items can be attained. For example, someone not

Table 4.1 MAS-A Scales and Anchors

Scale	*Levels*	*Characteristic Behavior Lower Scores*	*Characteristic Behavior Higher Scores*
Self-Reflectivity (S)	9	Fragmented sense of self with little to no sense that one is experiencing discernable mental activities	Self-experience integrated into a complex personal narrative with self seen as a unique and multifaceted being across the course of life
Understanding Others' Minds (O)	7	Fragmented sense of others with little to no sense that others experience discernable mental activities	Sense of others can be integrated into a complex narrative which joins different periods and experiences of that person across their life
Decentration (D)	3	No awareness that life events are not specifically related to oneself	Nuanced awareness that others have valid unique perspectives and relationships to one another
Mastery (M)	9	Gross inability to even frame an idea of a psychosocial challenge	Unique knowledge of the self, others, and the larger world is integrated and used to respond to real-life specific psychosocial challenges

capable of performing the metacognitive activity described by the fourth item of the MAS-A O scale (O4) would not be capable of performing the metacognitive activity described by the fifth item of the O scale (O5). The MAS-A has acceptable levels of interrater and test-retest reliability; extensive discussion of the MAS-A, its development, use, and psychometric properties can be found in Lysaker and Dimaggio (2014).

Significant MAS-A Findings

MAS-A and Severe Mental Illness

The development of a tool that assesses metacognition in a reliable and valid fashion has enabled us to better understand its role in severe mental illness. Consistent with our expectations, we found that persons with first episode and prolonged schizophrenia have significantly more metacognitive deficits as measured by the MAS-A than persons with other prolonged non-psychiatric medical conditions as well as individuals with a number of other conditions including substance abuse disorders (Lysaker, Leonhardt et al., 2014; Lysaker, Vohs et al., 2014; Vohs, Lysaker et al., 2014), borderline personality disorder (Lysaker et al., in press), minor anxiety and affective disorders (WeiMing et al., 2015a, 2015b), and healthy controls (Hasson-Ohayon et al., 2015; Popolo et al., 2017).

Other studies have documented the type and severity of metacognitive deficits found in other forms of serious mental illness including depression, posttraumatic stress disorder, and bipolar disorder differ (Ladegaard, Lysaker et al., 2014; Ladegaard, Larsen et al., 2014; Lysaker, Dimaggio et al., 2015; Popolo et al., 2017). These findings are important because they highlight how severe metacognitive impairments are not only associated with schizophrenia but also differ significantly from the types of metacognitive impairments seen in other mental illnesses and conditions. Here we found that persons with schizophrenia have both severe and widespread impairments in their integrative processes that are not seen in other conditions which are more focal and often less profound.

MAS-A and Clinical Course

Evaluating the impact of these deficits, other studies have found that having greater metacognitive deficits as measured with the MAS-A were related to greater disruptions in the ability to engage in a meaningful life (Lysaker & Dimaggio, 2014). Studies have found, for example, that impaired metacognitive function is associated with lower levels of functional competence (Lysaker, McCormick et al., 2011), a weaker subjective sense of recovery (Kukla et al., 2013), a weaker therapeutic alliance in a rehabilitation setting (Davis et al., 2011), decreased ability to deflect stigma (Nabors et al., 2014), a sedentary lifestyle (Snethen et al., 2014), difficulties in reasoning (Buck et al., 2012), anhedonia in the absence of depression (Buck et al., 2014), lower levels of intrinsic motivation (Luther et al., 2016a), and impulsive violence in forensic patients (Bo et al., 2014). Additionally, the relationship of metacognition and function persisted after controlling for indices of symptom severity and neurocognitive impairment in many of these studies.

It also appears that impaired metacognitive function can be linked with poorer quality of life regardless of the content of a person's cognitions about themselves (James et al., 2016). In other words, the complexity of ideas about the self and others affected function regardless of how positive or negative a person's thoughts were about themselves and others. As a result, the challenges these persons experience appear to be due to metacognitive deficits themselves and not a function of symptoms, dysfunctional beliefs, or cognitive impairments in general.

Additionally, metacognitive capacity predicts clinical outcomes. For example, higher levels of metacognitive capacity in adults with schizophrenia have been linked with better performance in a work rehabilitation program even after controlling for executive function (Lysaker, Dimaggio et al., 2010). Assessments of metacognition using the MAS-A also were associated with both current and future levels of negative symptoms (Hamm et al., 2012; Lysaker, Kukla, Dubreucq et al., 2015; McLeod et al., 2014). In each of these studies, lower scores on the MAS-A predicted higher levels of negative symptoms in the future after controlling for initial levels of symptoms. In other words, poorer metacognition appeared to be a risk factor for the emergence of more serious levels of negative symptoms. In a similar vein, other studies have found that poorer metacognition also predicted lower levels of intrinsic motivation in the future (Luther et al., 2016b; Vohs & Lysaker, 2014). Not surprisingly, factor analytic work suggests that metacognition measures a mental process that is distinct from social cognition and is linked with disturbances in behavior (Lysaker, Gumley et al., 2013). Finally, many of these findings have also been replicated in international settings including Italy (Nicolò et al., 2012), Turkey (Tas et al., 2012, 2014), French Canada (Massé & Lecomte, 2015), and Denmark (Trauelsen et al., 2016).

MAS-A and Response to Treatment

The MAS-A has also allowed us to begin to empirically explore whether metacognitive capacity can change in response to psychotherapy. Both detailed case work and an open psychotherapy trial have found that MAS-A scores improve over the course of both brief and longer-term therapies in adults with serious mental illness (de Jong et al., 2016; Leonhardt et al., 2016; Vohs & Leonhardt, 2016). A slightly different form of psychotherapy also targeting metacognition also led to significant increases in MAS-A scores (Bargenquast & Schweitzer, 2014; Bargenquast et al., 2015). There is also work documenting how

MAS-A scores taken monthly over the course of a period of two and a half years of psychotherapy show a long-term improvement in metacognition marked by a pattern of gains which are followed by short-term losses during times when pain emerges due to increased levels of awareness (Lysaker, Davis et al., 2005; Lysaker, Buck et al., 2007). This phenomenon will be discussed later when treatment is considered.

Summary

Using the MAS-A to quantify metacognition has led to several consistent findings. Prominent metacognitive deficits can be found in samples of adults in varying phases of illness. These deficits are also associated with immediate problems in psychological, social, and community function as well as the risk for future problems in these areas. Finally, metacognition appears to improve in response to treatment over time. These findings are important because they provide empirical support for MERIT's linkage of metacognitive impairment to severe mental illness. As a result, MERIT is not only consistent with other long-standing explanations of schizophrenia but is also rooted in contemporary science.

The MERIT Intervention Framework (MERIT-IF)

In order to assess metacognition during psychotherapy sessions and guide selection of the appropriate type of intervention, we also developed the MERIT Intervention Framework (MERIT-IF), a clinical tool which is an extension of the MAS-A. It uses three of MAS-A's four scales to guide interventions: Self-Reflectivity (S), Understanding Others' Minds (O), and Mastery (M), and retains the Decentration (D) scale for purposes of case conceptualization. The MERIT-IF will be discussed in detail in Chapter 12.

Section II

MERIT's Preconditions and Eight Core Elements

5 Preconditions for Implementing MERIT

MERIT provides an integrative framework for practitioners who work from a range of perspectives to direct the delivery of psychotherapy interventions that will lead to recovery by facilitating the growth of metacognitive capacity. We believe this methodology can assist therapists who work with persons with the full range of serious mental illnesses, both those who are experiencing very severe symptoms and those who are less impaired.

We assume that persons who are interested in learning to provide MERIT have already been trained in and are familiar with the fundamentals of providing psychotherapy. This includes understanding the relevant ethical and moral standards as well as the common factors of psychotherapy such as the need to establish a therapeutic alliance, maintain a non-judgmental stance, the importance of managing boundaries, and the criticality of being respectful of patients at all times.

While MERIT is not a rigid, prescriptive treatment methodology, the beliefs of therapists who implement it matter greatly. What a therapist expects can and should happen in treatment will influence how he attends to what patients say and what is understood. As such, this chapter will detail several specific ways of understanding serious mental illness that make the practice of MERIT possible. We refer to these as MERIT's preconditions. Each of these beliefs, or preconditions, bears upon how recovery is understood and the role both the patient and the therapist play in the process. It is critical that the therapist be comfortable with these principles because they provide the foundation for MERIT's recovery-oriented approach.

Precondition I: Recovery From Severe Mental Illness Is Possible

The first concept with which the MERIT therapist has to be comfortable is that people with serious mental illness can and do recover. This seemingly reasonable and non-controversial statement is well-supported by empirical research as well as first person reports (Davidson, 2003; Harding et al., 1987; Leonhardt et al., in press). However, while broadly accepted in the abstract, seeing recovery as a likely outcome for a specific individual being seen in treatment in the midst of an acute exacerbation or crisis is often more elusive. Sitting alone in a consulting office hour after hour with patients with serious mental illness can be disorganizing or even frightening for some therapists. Trying to understand the experience of someone who is in the midst of acute psychosis, paralyzed by pervasive hopelessness, or in a highly dysregulated state can be bewildering and intimidating. It is difficult to form ideas in one's own mind about the other when that other is actively experiencing the world as a chaotic and terrifying flow of unrelated fragments. This challenge is often compounded by both the tendency to attribute the behavior of others to enduring traits rather than situational factors and an often pervasive sense of pessimism about the course of mental illness. The result is that clinicians are often tempted to believe that the specific person before them can at best resolve her acute problems and achieve "stability" but is unable to actually recover and substantially improve the quality of her life. This is often reinforced by institutions where the explicit goal is to stabilize and transfer patients as quickly as possible to a lower level of care; unfortunately, the concept of long-term growth and improvement is not even considered because it is simply not part of the organization's thinking or mission.

Given both these pressures in the moment and the larger institutional zeitgeist, it is easy to see how clinicians can routinely lose sight that recovery can be an achievable and realistic goal. Additionally, patients themselves, who have often come to see themselves as helpless or perhaps even find some level of comfort or acceptance in a sick role, can encourage therapists, either implicitly or explicitly, to not see the potential for recovery in them. However, to consider recovery precludes the possibility of effectively delivering MERIT because it does not view stability or absence of acute distress as meaningful goals for treatment.

To accept that a unique person can recover requires complex metacognitive activity on the therapist's part. Seeing someone in a state of distress or profound disengagement from the world requires the formation of a complex idea about that person. The patient must be recognized as an individual who can experience widely different states over the course of her life which may include a successful premorbid period, grave current impairments, and the ability to have a satisfactory and rewarding life in the future. In this, wellness must be understood as more than the resolution of an acute problem and as participation in the world in a way that is not only free of disabling pain but is personally meaningful.

Maintaining the belief that recovery is real and likely for all patients is far from simple because the dynamics that promote recovery are poorly understood.

Persons can emerge from unfathomable levels of psychosis in ways that are not always anticipated. How and why symptoms will remit is not well understood, and the long-standing belief that wellness results from simply following orders and taking medication is not empirically supported (Harrow et al., 2014). While on the one hand MERIT therapists must accept the stance that recovery is possible, the path to it for each individual is uncertain and cannot be known ahead of time.

MERIT Precondition II: Patients Are Active Agents in Their Recovery

The second precondition is the belief that patients must be seen as active agents in their own recovery, both in terms of setting goals for treatment and determining how to achieve them. Here, MERIT embodies the concept of self-directed recovery (Davidson, 2005; SAMSA, 2005). As with the prior precondition that recovery is possible, therapists will often be familiar with the literature supporting the role of patients as active agents in their recovery (Davidson, 2003; Roe, 2001, 2005) and accept it in principle. However, therapists are often understandably made anxious when patients with serious mental illness are in the midst of acute psychosis, pervasively demoralized, or in a highly dysregulated state, provoking the clinician to take charge of the specific person in this specific circumstance.

Indeed, crises will inevitably emerge in work with severely impaired persons where firm action is needed such as when there is an acute risk for self-harm. However, what needs to be avoided is the insidious process by which therapists lose or fail to establish the idea that the specific person they are treating eventually *will* be able to seek and direct his own recovery. This dynamic is also reinforced by institutional concerns about risk management and patient safety which may lead clinicians to become preoccupied with any number of fantasized negative outcomes if they do not take control in a given situation. Additionally, as is the case where patients are not sure they can recover, patients and those around them may have also come to accept that they should not try to determine their own paths to recovery and that attempting to do so may lead to disaster.

MERIT is not a treatment that conceptualizes health as simply attaining "stability" or "diminishing short-term distress" as meaningful goals. Just as is the case with seeing recovery as a realistic outcome, accepting that a person can direct her own recovery also requires a complex metacognitive act on the part of the therapist. While therapists need to see the patient as a person with genuine struggles and some very real limitations that cannot be minimized, the patient also needs to be seen as capable of making sense of the psychiatric challenges she has faced and ultimately find a way to make life better for herself. For example, without losing sight of readily apparent neurocognitive deficits, symptoms, trauma history, previous self-destructive behaviors, poor choices, and interpersonal hostility, the therapist has to understand that patients can reflect upon their own experiences and determine what is personally meaningful to them and how they might choose to lead their lives.

In sum, therapists must form an ongoing and evolving multifaceted understanding of their patients. The presence of real limitations *and* the potential to understand and direct one's own life must be integrated within the therapist's understanding of patients. In the case of both the first and second preconditions, MERIT is not asking for therapists to stop being reflective and naively accept without question simple black or white assertions. The goal here is not to establish a "Pollyanna" view of profound disturbances in the lives of others. Indeed, not all patients will get better, and there is no reason to believe that MERIT will necessarily be able to help everyone. However, what each of these preconditions calls for is the belief that even the most confused patient can eventually be understood and can overcome profound barriers, ultimately finding ways to have a healthier life which is enriching for himself and others.

MERIT Precondition III: The Therapist's Role as Consultant and Equal Participant

The third basic understanding, closely tied to the first two, is that the patient-therapist relationship must be non-hierarchical. This is based upon the foundational belief that meaning-making is something constructed between two co-equals, not the result of a more powerful person directing or teaching someone who has less power.

Again, this is not always easy to achieve. Many patients have been socialized by the culture of mental health systems and the messages embedded in our larger social discourses that portray clinicians as more powerful and knowing than they are. Additionally, problems are often understood by patients and their families to result from "not listening to the doctor." Here, it is not uncommon to encounter a patient who relates a story in which she ignored medical advice, stopped taking a prescribed medication, experienced something undesirable, and then decided her judgment could no longer be trusted. As a result, people with such experiences often come to treatment with the expectation that they are going to be told how to recover.

Additionally, clinicians are in a more powerful position than patients in several ways, and this inevitably creates an unequal relationship. Clinicians often do possess professional expertise and the experience of having known many others who have struggled with serious mental illness. The therapist is paid, with sessions generally taking place in her office, and, if sufficiently alarmed, can take steps that will lead patients to being hospitalized against their will.

The result is that the power differential between the therapist and patient is real, and patients will often question their own judgment because of it. The key for the therapist is to assume the role of a consultant in the interaction with patients. Therapist reflections are offered as something for the patient to consider that may be accepted, rejected, or set aside because it is ultimately the patient's responsibility to decide how to respond to and use them. Similarly, it is expected that there will be negotiation, especially at the start of therapy, about what is to be discussed in treatment as well the therapist's role and boundaries of the relationship. Agreement on these points must be worked toward, not assumed *a priori* (Hasson-Ohayon & Lysaker, 2017).

MERIT also encourages therapists to consult with patients about the meaning they are making and not to attempt to "supply" it to them. Trying to provide solutions which patients can simply choose or reject is to be avoided as well as should trying to help the patient accept the "wiser" therapist's conceptualization of the problem. Consistent with other work on recovery, meaning-making occurs in the space between two persons and requires dialogue on an equal plane (Buck et al., 2015). As a result, this requires great sensitivity when offering thoughts so that they do not co-opt the meaning-making process. For example, if a patient were to report how ignoring a particular piece of advice led to a recent hospitalization, the therapist would not step in to offer a "truth" such as suggesting it is best to not ignore such advice in the future; instead the dyad might attempt to jointly understand the events and feelings leading up to the hospitalization. The process of sharing therapist reflections in a way that does not disrupt dialogue or joint meaning-making will be discussed in detail in Chapter 7 which explores the second MERIT element, inserting the mind of therapist into the treatment dialogue.

MERIT Precondition IV: The Experiences of Persons With Psychosis Can Be Understood

The fourth precondition is that psychotic experiences can be mutually understood by the therapist and patient. Positive, negative, and cognitive symptoms are often part of severe mental illness and will inevitably be evident during the course of psychotherapy sessions. The therapist's role is to treat all thoughts and experiences, including delusional material and thought disordered communications, as potentially meaningful, and these should not be ignored or extinguished before an understanding can be established. For instance, the emergence of an odd belief could be understood to have any of a number of potential meanings. From different perspectives, a persecutory delusion might be understood as an expression of fear trigged by an anomalous release of dopamine, a response to a threat to self-esteem, a wish to obliterate intersubjectivity, a fear of engulfment, an untrusting stance toward others that emerged in the wake of trauma, or distress cued by a therapist intervention.

This is consistent with findings that symptoms do not randomly emerge in psychotherapy sessions but can be tied to clear and understandable antecedents within the session (Leonhardt, Kukla et al., in press). This precondition also expects the therapist and patient to be continuously seeking to make meaning and resist the impulse for treatment to become symptom-focused. While a symptom could become the focus of treatment, this would only take place if its shared meaning were first developed (e.g., joint agreement that an automatic thought has become burdensome).

MERIT's position that psychosis is understandable deviates from many models of psychopathology, even including some European models of phenomenology which are highly concerned with understanding the patient's unique experience of the world. Similarly, other theoreticians argue that the self of a person with schizophrenia has become altered in a way such that it cannot be comprehended (Parnas, 2011) or is impaired to the point that the potential for intersubjectivity has been destroyed (Sass, 2000). MERIT categorically rejects these views. While self-disturbance is certainly evident in serious mental illness, it can be closely linked with understandable experiences of emotional pain (Hamm et al., 2015). In fact, clinical literature has long discussed (e.g. Searles, 1965) how, when these disturbances are understood and expressed in language, pain and symptomatology are reduced. This is also consistent with the observation that persons with schizophrenia act in ways "designed, no matter how obscurely, to accomplish something—it is goal directed," in all phases of illness (Will, 1967, p. 216). That being said, positive symptoms are rarely an effective means of expressing a thought or feeling. For instance, a persecutory delusion is often a rather ineffectual and tortured way to express feelings of fear and vulnerability. Nevertheless, symptoms are considered by a MERIT therapist as one potential mode of communication from one agentic being to another and considered to be a subject for reflection.

MERIT Precondition V: Greater Levels of Awareness May Lead to Emotional Distress

MERIT therapists need to be aware that the experience of increasing metacognitive capacity after a period of psychosis can be inordinately painful because patients may uncover or reconnect with additional sources of psychic distress as their recovery progresses. Buck et al. (2013) outlined a number of factors that contribute to this. First, some persons with serious mental illness have come to define themselves as "a mental patient" or "a schizophrenic" and see themselves in these terms. As a result, considering new ideas about who they are and what is possible in life may create significant dissonance. Degen and Nasper (1996) offer a compelling illustration in their description of a patient with schizophrenia who experienced very substantial improvement after trying a new medication but found this resulted in considerable anxiety because it challenged the previous views he had of himself: "Now I have to figure out what to do with the rest of my life . . . I want to be crazy . . . that's the only life I've known for years" (pp. 64–65). Buck et al. (2013) offer a similar example of a patient who experienced nostalgia for a familiar place in society as "one who had no responsibility" after his illness abated in response to metacognitively oriented psychotherapy.

In a similar vein, Buck et al. (2013) also suggest that increased metacognitive capacity may disrupt previous ways of making meaning because previous understandings of life challenges no longer retain their explanatory value. For example, a person who has developed a richer, more integrated sense of herself and others can no longer rely on paranoid interpretations of the events in her world. Likewise, a person who explained his unemployment in a delusional manner may feel bewildered and vulnerable when this goes away (Gilbert, 1989). Thus, the development of a more complex view of the world often brings the need to find newer and more complex understandings of the self.

Increased metacognitive capacity can also lead to a heightened awareness of losses that have been experienced, such as loved ones who are no longer part of their lives or relationships that have been strained to a point where repair is not possible without considerable risk. Patients may also become more aware of a trauma that triggered the emergence of psychosis or the trauma of psychosis itself, where the recognition of embarrassing or seemingly incomprehensible behavior in the past leads to a loss of previous self-confidence (Geekie, 2012). Additionally, some patients become acutely distressed by the realization of how episodes of acute symptomatology or emotional dysregulation have compromised interpersonal connections and negatively affected their ability and willingness to re-engage with others.

Awareness of these dynamics positions therapists to anticipate the need to foster an atmosphere that allows patients to feel safe experiencing and discussing pain in sessions (Liotti & Gilbert, 2011). Therapists must also be attentive to affective disturbances in patients and be willing to actively assist them to manage painful emotions by naming and discussing them as they emerge. The atmosphere of the session also needs to be such that both the therapist and patient can accept the patient's pain without alarm, grounded in the belief that pain can be understood and endured in the context of a compassionate exchange with others.

In summary, clinicians need to be aware that greater awareness of oneself and others may lead in any number of unexpected directions and that the emergence of pain is not necessarily a sign of failure in the treatment but a natural and growth-promoting consequence. As a result, clinicians need to be continually curious and reflective about what is happening in sessions because progress is unlikely to be simple or to follow a linear pattern. Ultimately, as with the previous preconditions, the challenge for therapists is to form more complex and integrated ideas of patients without resorting to simple formulaic concepts about patients and their responses to treatment.

MERIT Precondition VI: Social Stigma Can Profoundly Impact Persons With Severe Mental Illness

The final precondition is that therapists need to remain continuously attuned to the presence of stigma and its impact upon persons with mental illness. Stigma refers to widely held negative social beliefs about persons with mental illness and may include frank assertions that they are more prone to violent and disorderly behavior, lack personal competence, are unable to work, or are incapable of making informed decisions (Markowitz, 1998; Martin et al., 2000; Phelan et al., 2000). Stigma can be embedded in a wide range of unexpected situations including humor, media reports which highlight the mental health history of criminals regardless of its relevance, and in seemingly benign verbalizations such as a remark that a mentally ill man is "cute" which may have an infantilizing quality.

From a psychotherapeutic standpoint, stigma is especially important for MERIT because it may incline persons with schizophrenia to accept the negative images of themselves that are prevalent in social discourse. It may also stimulate self-fulfilling prophecies of failure (Firmin et al., in press; Lysaker et al., 2007; Yanos et al., 2008, 2010) and work at counter purposes with forming a more complex understanding of the self. This environment also requires therapists to be aware of their own potentially stigmatizing views including the covert stigma that might be found in seemingly benign interventions such as expecting less competency of patients than they do of others or of themselves.

Stigma may also appear in therapists' attitudes when they are less interested in patients' own understanding of life events and become more concerned that they accept that they are experiencing a disorder or illness. Such a stance not only co-opts meaning-making but also embodies an implicit stigmatizing message that patients can only understand their lives if they accept the clinician's vision that they are mentally ill. The key issue regarding insight into mental illness is not that therapists have to suspend their own beliefs that the patient has a psychiatric disorder. However, they do need to recognize how the patient is fully entitled to make sense of his own condition and that a dialogue about the meanings the patient assigns to what others have labeled as "his illness" is possible.

Summary

This chapter described six basic ideas that therapists need to be fully comfortable with before they can truly understand how to practice MERIT. Each

Table 5.1 Preconditions for MERIT

MERIT's Preconditions	
I	The patient as a unique person can recover.
II	The patient as a unique person is the only person who can direct his or her path to recovery.
III	The conversations which support recovery must be non-hierarchical.
IV	Disorganized or unusual material which emerges in the dialogue can be understood.
V	Enhanced metacognition can result in heightened emotional pain.
VI	Stigma is present in the mind of everyone and must be continuously assessed and countered.

of these six preconditions call for therapists to be prepared to form increasingly complex ideas about patients and create a therapeutic context in which patients come to form more complex understandings of themselves and their lives (see Table 5.1).

6 Overview of MERIT's Elements and Element 1

The Agenda

Overview of MERIT's Elements

MERIT's clinical practice is defined by eight elements or processes which guide a therapist in delivering psychotherapy designed to assist adults with serious mental illness to recapture impaired or undeveloped metacognitive abilities. These are summarized in Table 6.1.

The first four elements of MERIT are *content* elements and pertain to what is discussed in each session. They describe the process of naming a different facet of the patient's experience and making it the subject for reflection. Like a jigsaw puzzle, each element describes how a new piece, or fragment of experience, can be identified and later integrated into a more complex view of the self and others and used by the patient to decide how to respond to life's challenges. The second set of elements describe the *process* by which sessions are carried out while the third set are the *superordinate* elements which describe *what* MERIT is seeking to facilitate. While all of the elements are interrelated, each must be considered specifically and individually, and therapists are expected to attend to all elements as the session progresses.

Each element will be discussed and accompanied by a review of the corresponding dimension of MERIT Therapist Adherence Scale (MERIT-TAS),

Table 6.1 MERIT Elements

	MERIT's Elements	*Type*
1	Preeminent focus on the patient agenda	Content
2	Insertion of the therapist's mind	Content
3	Eliciting narrative episodes	Content
4	Eliciting the psychological problem	Content
5	Reflection on the therapeutic relationship	Process
6	Reflection upon progress	Process
7	Stimulating reflections about the self and others	Superordinate
8	Stimulating reflections about mastery	Superordinate

a tool designed to help clinicians measure how well they are implementing each element. A copy of the MERIT-TAS can be found in Appendix II.

MERIT Element 1: The Agenda

MERIT Element 1 requires the therapist to focus and reflect with patients about their agenda—what they are seeking, including the wishes, hopes, and plans they bring to the session. Multiple agendas are possible and may be unrelated to or contradictory with each other. An agenda is the product of the patient's momentary and persistent intentions, motives, aims, goals, and needs, and implies it is the patient who determines the goals of treatment.

This element necessitates joint reflection about what lies beneath the patient's actions or verbalizations in the moment. Neither intended to lay out a formal protocol to structure the session like a business meeting nor to find the patient's "true" agenda, the goal of seeking the agenda is to think together with patients about what they hope results from the session. Some examples of agendas may include:

- To feel less anxious
- To establish something is not their fault
- To make the therapist feel confused
- To convince the therapist to agree with their estimation of another person
- To feel safe
- To feel connected to someone
- To be rejected by the therapist
- To be admired by the therapist
- To please the therapist
- To seek permission to give up
- To decide how to respond to a loss
- To avoid a drug relapse

The focus on the agenda positions the patient as an agentic being with recognizable needs, hopes, wishes, and desires in the moment that can be named and, therefore, be the subject of reflection. It also places joint reflection about what is happening in the mind and body of the patient at the forefront of the therapeutic exchange. This means that the gaze of the therapist and patient are always returning to the experiences of the patient. This ensures that the central focus will remain on parts of experience that might later be integrated to form larger, more complex representations of the self and others.

Complexity of the Agenda

As has been described elsewhere (Hamm, Buck, Leonhardt et al., in press), patients will generally have more than one recognizable agenda which may vary significantly from each other. Patients may be aware of their agendas before the session begins, arriving with a certain set of wishes or intentions to share or discuss. Alternately, they may come to the session with little sense of what they are seeking and may even be surprised as their agendas emerge as the conversation unfolds. Like all human desires, agendas may be healthy or unhealthy and more or less internally consistent. Patients' agendas can sometimes be clearly and readily discernable in the moment. Other times these agendas can remain quite opaque. Given that multiple agendas are likely to be present, therapists can expect to encounter agendas that at various times will complement or contradict one another, or that will be completely unrelated. The patient's agendas are also likely to change across the course of the session, and an initial agenda may be replaced with others as the session progresses.

Regardless of the similarity of content, patient agendas can also differ in terms of how they position the therapist within the therapy relationship. Three patients who are overwhelmed with feelings of failure and inadequacy could seek relief in different ways within a given session. One might overtly seek reassurance or compassion from the therapist in order to feel more adequate. The second could criticize the therapist in the hope of making her feel inept, thereby making the patient feel less inadequate. A third patient might broach an irrelevant topic to distract the therapist to hide from painful feelings until they were forgotten.

Agendas May Not Be Immediately Apparent

It is not unusual for patients to come to the session and be unable to identify what they are seeking. Indeed, some struggle to state their agenda clearly even after considerable experience in psychotherapy. Consider the patient who comes to a session hoping to be relieved of guilt for an argument with a partner, wanting to feel less inept as a person and recapture a sense of safety. He is unlikely to clearly state: "I'm here to make it clear I'm not guilty for the argument I just had with my partner, to feel less inadequate, and to recapture a sense of safety." He is more likely to sit down and say things such as: "My partner is so cold and selfish, and, by the way, you aren't helping me as much as my last therapist," or perhaps, "I have to ask you, so were you following me last night?!"

Here, the therapist's task is to think with patients about what it means when they say each of these things and explore what the patient is seeking when he says: "My partner is so cold and selfish." The patient may share how the partner appeared distant after the conflict, leading to the joint conclusion that the one thing the patient wants from this session is a pronouncement that he is not at fault for the altercation and to alleviate his guilt over it. In addressing the patient's criticisms of the therapist, it might be established that the patient wanted the clinician to feel inept and to know what it is like for the patient to feel inept. Finally, when the therapist thinks about the patient's question about whether she was following him, it might be discovered that the patient has been feeling unsafe recently and is wanting the therapist to offer a reassuring statement that will help to re-establish his sense of security. Of course, there may be other agendas linked to these utterances as well. The principle embodied in this element is that therapists and patients must seek the larger intentions and motives that may lie behind a specific utterance.

Helping Patients to Clarify Their Agendas

The initial steps in detecting an agenda require the therapist to attend to the patients' verbal and non-verbal behaviors throughout the session. A range of agendas may be expressed by a patient's comments or demeanor in the waiting room. A scowl or an unusual greeting can offer a clue about the patient's emotional state and what he might be seeking as well as might his first words. It is important that the therapist recognize that any number of intentions may lie beneath a simple utterance, and that the patient can use the same words from session to session and yet express different intentions each time.

In order to illustrate how multiple agendas can be present in an utterance, Table 6.2 lists several agendas which potentially might be expressed in either of two simple opening patient comments: "I am hearing voices" and "What

Table 6.2 Potential Agendas Expressed by a Simple Utterance

I am hearing voices.	*What have you been reading lately?*
Know I am suffering.	Can you talk to me like I'm a normal person?
Help me to be calm.	Can we avoid silence?
Don't expect a lot of me.	Know that I don't feel like I know you.
Help me avoid a crisis in my life (by focusing on this problem).	Can I get to know you so you are not so scary?
Don't notice I am doing drugs.	Don't notice I am doing drugs.
Notice I am doing drugs.	Notice I am doing drugs (because I am bringing up an irrelevant topic).
Help me feel safe.	Let's not talk about an earlier subject (by focusing on this).
Understand that I feel completely alone.	Show me how you will act if I surprise you.
Let's not talk about an earlier subject (by focusing on this problem).	Ask me more about myself.
Don't harm me because I am vulnerable.	I am not sure what I should be interested in.
Praise me (because I am playing the role of a psychiatric patient).	I want to avoid talking about something painful on my mind.
I want to give you (the therapist) something to do (fix this problem).	I would like to know what you think about when you are alone.
Help me manage this symptom.	Are you willing to share too?
Let's not talk about something painful on my mind (by focusing on this problem).	I would like to feel intelligent when we talk.
The voices are controlling my behavior, not me, so don't hold me responsible.	

book are you reading?" Additionally, any number of these may all be accurate at the same time, and the underlying meaning of the same utterance may change from session to session.

Therapists can utilize a number of mental processes in order to move from observing a patient's speech and behavior to facilitating the development of a shared agenda. First, therapists might consider their own intuition and immediate reactions to what takes place in sessions. After a patient speaks, the therapist should be aware of her own somatic and affective reactions. Does she notice a change in her own mental states? As the patient talks about the fear of being followed, does the therapist find herself becoming bored, or irritated, or identify a sense of fear the patient will scold her if she interrupts the patient? Second, therapists also may feel impelled to take a certain action. As the patient talks about his or her partner, does the therapist feel pulled to make critical and judgmental comments about that partner? When the patient tells the therapist about the voice he hears, does the therapist feel inclined to offer a lecture about how to respond to voices or think she should inhibit the wish to ask about a significant conflict discussed in the last session?

Therapists' reflections may also be based upon what they know about a given patient or persons in general who suffer from the same condition. Knowledge of the patient's lifelong pattern of feeling guilty for conflict or tendencies to belittle others to relieve feelings of inadequacy could provide clues about the meaning of the utterances. Does the patient have a history of seeking distraction when he feels he is ready to relapse and buy cocaine? Does the patient view his own knowledge from reading academic books as one of his only strong points? Additionally, therapists may try to remember times when they have acted in ways that were similar to how the patient is acting and base a reflection related to their own experiences in those moments. When have they complained about a partner or criticized someone, and when they did so, what did they intend? Similarly, what was the underlying meaning when they focused on a symptom or asked someone what she was reading?

Such therapist activities will give rise to a number of potential agendas to consider that can be further refined as the patient says more and reacts to what the therapist says and does as part of the therapeutic dialogue. Patient responses to therapist actions such as silence, questions, reflections, or interpretations will also often give more information. For example, if the therapist is silent, does the patient begin to protest even more fervently about the coldness of her partner, or does the she begin to cry? Does the patient ignore the therapist after the therapist offers a reassuring comment? Does the patient quickly change the subject, sigh in relief, or angrily fall silent after a therapist offers a thought about how to cope with an auditory hallucination?

Here, understanding or grasping the patient's agenda is not a passive process in which the therapist should accept what is offered at face value. Therapists should further not confine themselves to offering reflections about what the patient has said. At times, they will need to make direct inquiries to better understand what the patient is seeking. More often than not, therapist action is likely to be needed to understand what the patient intends and wants. The therapist should not wait but venture out and begin inquiring about what the patient has in mind in the moment. This kind of therapist activity both assists the therapist to understand the agenda and also communicates to the patient the therapist's interest in her, even if the initial understanding of the patient's agenda is not accurate. Recognizing that the therapist is a unique person, these deeply subjective responses will inevitably vary according to the clinician's theoretical background, type of experience, individual characteristics, and personal background.

Importance of a Shared Process

Finding the patient's agenda is also not a matter of the therapist deciding, interpreting, or discovering what should be done for the patient nor is it a passive process in which the patient accepts what the therapist offers at face value. Rather, there must be shared reflection about what the patient is seeking from the session. In other words, there should be an iterative process where there is a smooth and continuous interplay between the therapist listening and observing, monitoring his own reactions, offering a reflection, then thinking together with the patient about her response.

Throughout this shared process, there is no need for the patient to accept a reflection. Rather, there is only a need for joint acknowledgment that the patient is seeking a certain thing in the moment. The goal of this element is fostering the process of joint reflection about potential intentions in the moment, not in finding the "true" agenda. As long as there has been consideration of different potential agendas, this element is considered to have been achieved, even if a joint understanding of an agenda does not emerge in a session.

What Hinders Detection of the Agenda

While there are likely innumerable ways in which therapists and patients can fail to understand one another, there are some common challenges when clinicians are learning to practice MERIT. The first and foremost is for the therapist to take verbalizations at face value and ignore the subtleties and hints inherent during sessions. Since therapists are often socialized to "like" their patients and to advocate for them, it may seem like a violation of this role if the therapist notices potentially unseemly aspects of an agenda. It may also feel more benevolent and appropriate to assume that the agenda behind "I am hearing a voice" is to find a way to eliminate that experience rather than, perhaps, to garner support for fulfilling the patient role or unsettle the clinician. Similarly, it may feel like a betrayal when the therapist detects envy or sadism in a patient's behavior. However, if the therapist believes that forming a negative idea about the patient is somehow inappropriate and insulting, he will be unable to accomplish the task of developing increasingly more complex and integrated ideas about the patient.

Stigma may also position therapists to view patients as different from other people and lead to misunderstanding their intentions. If mentally ill adults are seen as people who are essentially simpler and less complicated, therapists may profoundly underestimate the reality that the agendas of mentally ill persons are as perplexing and contradictory as anyone else's. This may also blind them to common human wishes for revenge or power. Further, if stigma leads therapists to believe that mentally ill adults are fundamentally different kinds of people than others or themselves, it impairs clinicians' abilities to use their own experience to understand the patient's agenda. Here, if therapists see patients as fundamentally unlike them, they cannot use their own experiences of, for example, rejection or lack of status, as a basis for thinking about the agenda of a highly paranoid patient.

Another barrier is failing to start the session in way that facilitates emergence of the agenda. MERIT suggests sessions be started by asking patients, "Where do you want to start?" and avoiding other interaction until the patient responds; failing to do so risks missing important clues. Not allowing patients to start sessions where they wish may also make it difficult for them to express or experience their agenda. Similarly, neglecting to pay attention to a patient's behavior from the outset may be invalidating, as it implicitly detracts from the process of letting patients experience what they think, feel, desire, and strive for in the moment as important.

Other behaviors that block the joint understanding of an agenda include a medicalized stance which renders therapists unable to see symptom descriptions or problem reports as anything but direct requests for help or therapists assuming a defensive posture exemplified by simplistic statements like the patient "wants to manipulate me" or "lacks motivation." MERIT holds that all humans have basic needs which include attachment, social rank, sexuality, and threat-detection (Liotti & Gilbert, 2011). Resultantly, the behavior of patients is driven by human motives, and these motives need to be understood. For example, a patient may reject warmth on the part of the therapist and make a seemingly manipulative request because of his experiences where several others who expressed warmth had sexually molested him. Another patient may reject a job, not because of lack of motivation, but because the rewards of remaining in the patient role are more tangible and familiar.

From the MERIT perspective, if therapists describe patients as "manipulative" and "lacking motivation," this often reflects a therapist agenda concerned with controlling rather than understanding and driven by feelings of confusion or frustration with the patient. In a similar vein, therapists must be wary about accepting simplistic or likely disingenuous agendas such as: "I just want to vent" and "I just want support." Patients who say such things do have agendas, but they are undoubtedly more complex than these utterances express at the surface level.

Finally, while there is not a clear-cut way to discern where any behavior falls on the continuum of disingenuous to genuine, there are therapists' reactions that may signal an overly simple agenda has been accepted, such as when therapists find themselves overtly encouraging or "cheering" for patients rather than thinking with them or acknowledging feelings of exhaustion or irritation at the end of sessions. Additionally, the therapist's experience that agendas are completely unconnected from week to week with little integration is also a sign that a disingenuous agenda may have been accepted as authentic.

Clinical Illustrations

Consider the patient who sat down and immediately noted the temperature was "warm" in the office. The therapist found herself wondering if this was a part of an agenda related to the patient's feeling uncomfortable being with her in the office or potentially about something he was confronting in his life. The therapist also wondered if this was small talk intended to lead somewhere else or a simple request to adjust the thermostat. The therapist then noticed that she did not feel warm and that the temperature seemed to be at the usual level. She sought for a memory of feeling quite warm herself and could recall having that sensation before having to perform at a piano recital.

The patient talked a little more about the temperature, which the therapist thought might be significant but was unsure about what the patient wanted her to think. The therapist remained silent, and the patient finally said that he suddenly realized he was anxious. The therapist asked him to say more, and the patient first talked in generalities and abstractions and asked if they could talk about coping skills. The therapist was silent and then the patient disclosed that he was going on a trip to see family in another part of the country. The therapist directly asked him whether he was telling her that he was anxious about the trip. The patient concurred and went on to describe his recent experience of paranoid thoughts and visual hallucinations.

At this point, the therapist decided that this was not small talk but the patient's agenda about anxiety over an upcoming visit. She was also aware of her own creeping sense of boredom with the discussion coupled with an inclination to help excuse the patient from having to make this trip. An exploration of the trip yielded only cursory information that offered little sense of the patient's subjective experience, leading her to feel confused when the patient went on to say that he actually did want to go on this trip where several siblings and their families would be present. The therapist's next thought was that she did not experience any enthusiasm herself for the trip nor did the patient, despite his statements to the contrary.

However, she was struck that something felt insincere about the patient's request for coping skills and subsequently formed the idea that the patient's direct request for "coping skills" reflected his wish to not talk about the source of anxiety. Again, feeling the impulse to tell the patient he did not have to go on the trip, she was also aware in the moment that he frequently had used somatic complaints as a rationale to drop college courses when he was not performing well. This led her to the hypothesis that the patient was anxious and wanted to escape his anxiety by positioning her to tell him he was too "sick" to go on this trip. In response, the therapist validated the patient's anxiety but directly asked if his goal was not so much for her to help him feel calmer but instead find a way to avoid the trip. The patient laughed, thinking aloud about how this was indeed what he was seeking. The therapist playfully noted that she had better not teach coping skills or the patient would have to go on the trip. Again, the patient laughed and agreed he wanted to avoid this trip because he felt so inadequate around his siblings and that he was trying to avoid that pain rather than having to deal with it.

In this example, the patient and therapist are thinking together about what the patient is seeking, and they move quickly to a poignant set of dilemmas. The patient is also an active agent with recognizable mental states and an agenda. He wanted to feel less inadequate. Of course, any number of other agendas could have been found within this initial utterance with other patients. For example, with another patient, it might have been discovered that comments about the office being warm were part of an agenda that involved discussing how inattentive the therapist had been to the patient's needs, where mentioning the office temperature was a lead in to discuss how inhospitable discussions with the therapist often feel. Another patient might have intended this utterance to let the therapist know she was not in any state to be pressured today, where "feeling warm" might have meant she was in a fragile state and the therapist would be inconsiderate to confront her with a subject she wanted to avoid that day. Another patient could have been expressing that the office was warm and comfortable, and hence a safe and hospitable place. And if matters were not already too complicated, multiple agendas might all be operative at the same time. The point is that the therapist's attention and focus must sift through what is happening to think about what patients are genuinely seeking.

As a second illustration, consider the patient who sat down and said: "I have dead people in my belly" and then was silent. The therapist was aware that he felt confused and unsettled by the statement and so found himself choosing to say nothing. After a few moments, he formed the idea that the patient was trying to express something about an internal experience, albeit in a disorganized manner. He imagined that internal experience might involve the patient having feelings of deadness or the intrusion of memories of persons who are dead. He imagined that the patient also might have used these words to make him feel disorganized in order to avoid any intersubjective connection from the outset of the session.

Next, he tried to imagine a time when he had a potentially similar sensation and at best could come up with an image of having difficulties digesting the idea a close friend had betrayed him years ago. When the patient changed topics, the therapist decided he had to take some kind of action in order to begin discovering with the patient what she wanted. He asked directly about the experience the patient might be trying to express and queried if having dead persons in her stomach was distressing and, if so, how much? What was the sensation like? Was this a feeling that was blocking discussion of something else? Her responses shed little light and the therapist did not feel any less confused. Moreover, the patient appeared to be in little distress with affect that bordered on inappropriately bright.

The therapist called to mind the last session when the patient seemed enthused about the possibility of getting a job for the first time in years. This led him to form a new idea: the patient was both trying to say she had lost her enthusiasm for work and to erase from the therapist's mind last week's determination to work because of the potential humiliation associated with doing so. He said, "So, it is important. You want me to know that you have decided not to work?" The patient looked puzzled but her affect noticeably changed with a hint of distress in her face. He added, "You want me to forget about work. Maybe I should know you feel too sick and dead inside to try that." In response, the patient began to have tears and shook her head in agreement. She went on to note that she feared failure if she tried to work again and that while she wanted to be more active, it felt too unsafe to try.

In both illustrations, one with a relatively unremarkable utterance and another with one that was seemingly incomprehensible, a clearly discernible set of human intentions was discerned. Of course, alternative chains of responses were possible with the patient finding that the therapist reflections were inaccurate, as indeed they may have been. If so, therapist would simply acknowledge that the patient's agenda remained unclear and begin the process again.

MERIT-TAS Element 1

The MERIT Therapist Adherence Scale (MERIT-TAS) Element 1 scale can be found in Table 6.3. As noted in the table, satisfactory adherence to this element requires either multiple attempts to make the agenda manifest across the session or a significant joint discussion about the patient's agenda. Optimal level of adherence requires both frequent attempts to elicit the agenda and a significant discussion about that agenda.

Table 6.3 MERIT-TAS Element 1 Scale

Score	*Level of Adherence*	*Therapist Behavior*
0	Absent	Failure to make the patient's agenda manifest
1	Marginal	Singular or infrequent attempts to make the agenda manifest without a significant statement emerging about the patient's agenda
2	Satisfactory	Frequent attempts to make the agenda manifest **or** a significant statement which emerges about the patient's agenda
3	Optimal	Frequent attempts to make the agenda manifest **and** a significant statement which emerges about the patient's agenda

7 Element 2

Insertion of the Therapist's Mind

MERIT's Element 2 is "insertion of the therapist's mind" which asks clinicians to share their own thoughts and reactions to the patient's behaviors and mental activities in a way that does not derail dialogue or co-opt the patient's agenda(s). The intent of this is twofold. First, it establishes the therapist as a person with her own distinct thoughts and reactions who is available and present for dialogue and joint reflection. Second, it establishes the patient as someone who has reactions to the therapist as a partner in dialogue. As Element 1 allows for patients to be aware of different intentions and motives they themselves possess, Element 2 allows for patients to be aware of the different reactions they have in response to a person in their immediate presence who is thinking about them with them.

Examples of inserting the therapist's mind may include sharing that:

- The patient is smiling while describing things that are generally frightening
- The therapist is confused by what the patient is saying
- The therapist notices the patient is wearing dark glasses or an odd orange hat
- The therapist is hearing things from the patient that make her feel anxious
- The therapist feels if he says the wrong thing, it will anger the patient
- The patient has not spoken of the crisis that was the subject of the last session
- The subject has not arisen that the patient failed to attend the last two sessions without cancelling
- The therapist is thinking something different

This necessitates a nuanced process that asks therapists to genuinely share what is happening in their minds while still fostering mutual understanding and joint reflection. It is not concerned with therapists "getting it right" and sharing the "correct" thoughts but rather in forming a connection in which two minds can cooperate and reflect upon the experience of that cooperation in all its vicissitudes. These different reactions can also then be explored and integrated into a more complex sense of self and others, a key process in MERIT's vision of recovery.

Basic Conditions for Sharing the Therapist's Thoughts

While perhaps an obvious point, the kinds of thoughts therapists should share is in part dependent upon the degree of trust which has been established between the patient and therapist. How and when therapists share a potentially challenging thought or reaction should be tempered by whether the patient feels safe with the therapist and the extent to which it might be viewed as a threat rather than an attempt to understand. The therapist's knowledge of the patient's background should also be a guide to the sort of language that will be meaningful as well as when and how ideas should be communicated. Problems, painful emotional states, and patterns across a lifetime should be discussed in plain and non-theoretical language. In the eyes of MERIT, treatment is never a matter of teaching people to use a new language or to adopt a particular psychological perspective.

The therapist's thoughts must be offered with explicit concern for their potential impact upon the patient's ownership of the session's agenda. While psychotherapy is a dialogue, it is a dialogue that takes place on the therapist's "turf" where the clinician possesses far more power than the patient. As an example, if conflicting agendas are not addressed and handled delicately through sharing the therapist's thoughts, patients will nearly always find themselves in a subordinate position and either defiantly resist or begrudgingly acquiesce to the therapist's thoughts, in both cases halting mutual reflection. To illustrate this dilemma, consider the patient whose agenda is to seek the therapist's endorsement of a plan to invest what little money she has in pyramid scheme and use the proceeds to purchase a luxury car. To avoid overriding her agenda while still expressing his concern, the therapist first verbalized the patient's agenda. He then went on to share his worries about her losing all her money as well as the impact of these comments upon the patient. Alternatively, consider the patient who shares his concern that his family is plotting against him and plans to confront them at a family picnic. Here, there would be two competing agendas: the patient's wish to share his anger with his family and the therapist's wish to help the patient avoid an outburst that would further alienate him from family. In response, the therapist might again first acknowledge the patient's agenda and then ask whether she could share her concern that this would confuse or drive his family away rather than lead to greater understanding.

It bears repeating that insertion of the therapist's mind does not ask that things be discerned with absolute accuracy. Indeed, if a therapist says she is having a certain thought, then that represents an accurate statement if she is indeed having that thought. What is important is that therapists form multiple ideas and express them with sensitivity by carefully assessing their impact within the context of the discussion, the degree of trust within the relationship, and the patient's background. This may feel threatening to the therapist's own cognitive operations or the wish to feel in control. Especially in the early stages of the relationship, it may necessitate careful trial and error and the clinician's vigilance for interventions that may derail the dialogue. This requires continuous willingness by therapists to see their own thoughts and reflections as potentially fallible and likely to be ill-timed and even wrong at points. Nonetheless, the insertion of the therapist's mind is offered as an attempt to understand which is intended to be helpful to the patient.

The Therapist's Stance

One metaphor to consider for Element 2 of MERIT is that the therapist is establishing a beachhead, one in which her mind is established as being present despite the possibility that the patient is ambivalent about that presence. This requires an open, non-controlling, and non-threatening inquisitive stance which allows the patient to freely move to other streams of discourse without coming into conflict with what the therapist may wish. Managing this requires the continuous monitoring of a number of dynamics that are themselves in flux. As a result, the therapist has to be continuously thinking with the patient, present in the dialogue, and sensitive to activities which seem to open or close dialogue, a complex task that likely can never be done perfectly.

Such an open stance places the therapist in a position of wanting to understand the experience of the patient. What is shared must be from an interest in what the patient will say without any clear idea of the outcome. However, it can be difficult for clinicians to maintain such an open stance because they are often trained and socialized to "fix" things and frequently harbor the belief that they need to "get" patients to do or think certain things. These non-open stances can take a number of different forms and have been detailed in several sources (e.g., Hamm, Buck, Vohs et al., in press) and are common when clinicians are learning to use MERIT. As a result, it is important for clinicians to be aware of them.

One common non-open stance is the *arbiter of reality*. Emerging from the awareness that many persons with serious mental illness have deeply improbable beliefs that are at odds with adaptive responses to the environment, therapists can come to believe their primary job is to correct this. As a result, if patients get reality "right," the therapist thinks they will be in a better position to improve their lives. This can lead therapists to share thoughts not for the purposes of joint reflection but to make sure the patient knows what is real and what is not. This puts the clinician in the position as the "one who knows" and in the role of coaxing or teaching the other to accept this knowledge. For example, when a patient comes to therapy with the hope that it will appease his persecutors so they will not kill him, the arbiter of reality might tell the patient he is having a delusion and take on the responsibility of orienting him to a "more objective" way of seeing things. By contrast, a therapist with an open stance would try to first understand the person who is having the experience of the delusion rather than addressing its likelihood. When clinicians position themselves in a way that they are the better judge of reality within the dyad, they not only derail dialogue but also place the patient in a helpless and passive position.

Another non-open position is the *spokesperson* who openly advocates for the patient. In light of movements such as positive psychology (Seligman et al., 2006), therapists may urge patients to have hope and courage and feel they should broadly praise these attitudes, no matter the context. The wish to advocate for persons with severe mental illness may feel natural, if not an absolute requirement, given the considerable adversity they experience. The spokesperson may say he is simply pursuing the best interests of the patient from a place that emphasizes the patient's strengths. By his actions, he seeks to empower patients and make them more capable, positioning himself as responsible for that. However, the problem with this stance in both examples is that clinicians take on the position of speaking for patients rather than talking with them.

Consider the patient who is angry with himself after leaving an event at his church due to a panic attack. The spokesperson may suggest strategies for thinking about the problem or share her thoughts about how the content of the event might have reasonably upset the patient so it was only natural that he would want to leave. However, quickly taking this stance may lead the clinician to not explore the events that occurred—say, that the patient lingered in the parking lot for some time after he left in the hope that others would ask him what had happened, which would miss the opportunity to explore a whole new set of meanings. Similarly, in the face of family conflict, the spokesperson might speculate about the legitimacy of the patient's anger at family members while not considering it might be related to the patient's difficulties detecting emotional warmth in others. Thus, there may be a tendency in this case for the therapist to deny the presence of hostility and aggression in order to accentuate the positive, which can invalidate the patient's basic psychological experiences. Here, the therapist may possess avowed empathy for the patient and even assume a blanket faith in the patient's strength but does so without any nuanced understanding of who the patient is as a unique being in the world. In contrast, an open position leads the clinician to focus on understanding the person who is suffering, rather than ameliorating the suffering itself.

A third non-open stance is the *ambassador of health* in which therapists share "healthy" practices they have discovered to be beneficial to either themselves or others and then indiscriminately encourage patients to share in their benefit. For instance, when meeting with the patient who fled a church meeting, the ambassador of health might be inclined to direct the conversation to his favorite practice (e.g., "breathe deeply and think peaceful thoughts") but inadvertently ignore exploring the patient's negative feelings at the time and/or the patient's strengths that were also evident (e.g., he drove across town for the meeting and participated in the preliminary social event).

While providing this type of advice is not categorically unhelpful, it does not come from a position of understanding and may prevent exploring how patients might find safety and meaning in their unhealthy behaviors. For instance, aggressive outbursts may be a patient's sole source of power and have to be carefully understood and empathized with and not simply seen as a sign of ill health that will fade with time. The ambassador of health position, regardless of its good intentions, makes the therapist the benevolent guide which robs the dyad of a chance for understanding one another as human beings who are facing difficulties that may seem very challenging at times. Speaking from a position aligned with promoting healthy perspectives may also limit opportunities for patients to become more aware of their own conflictual stances and how they might choose to react to them.

The fourth non-open position is that of *minister of comfort* where therapists see their role as largely being in the service of diminishing patients' pain. An image this calls to mind is that of a caretaker offering a blanket and hot tea to a shivering person who has come in from the cold. People with serious mental illnesses truly suffer and not wanting to alleviate their pain would seem inhumane. The open stance, though, is interested in the nature of that pain and how it has been experienced and is being expressed by a unique and complex individual.

Consider the patient who has fled the church meeting or felt shunned at the family gathering. The minister will offer thoughts and reactions as a kind of balm that will reduce distress. This could include noting how the therapist is struck by the patient's level of distress or offering other thoughts which are little more than empathic overtures. Indeed, as with virtually every other model of psychotherapy, MERIT necessitates an empathic attitude. The critical factor for MERIT, though, is the position from which it is offered. Empathic utterances with the primary goal of removing the pain without an overriding concern with its meaning are not truly expressions of empathy but more of a masquerade where the patient may come to feel better but be left with little to reflect upon or learn from. A very real danger in this dynamic is that it expresses or is driven by a stigmatizing mentality on the part of the therapist which positions people with schizophrenia as unstable in the face of pain or at the least unable to develop a rich meaningful life and only hope for relief from a benevolent but ultimately patronizing other. This stance also neglects the fact that all patients may not necessarily want the pain to stop immediately but are rather driven by the desire to feel connected to the therapist and be understood.

Insertion of the Therapist's Mind From an Open Stance

The commonality shared by each of these non-open stances is *the intention of the therapist to do something more than understand.* The arbiter wants to establish what is real and not real. The spokesperson wants to advocate for the patient. The ambassador wants to get the patient healthy. The minister wants to see a reduction in distress. While all socially appropriate, each facilitates the formation of a hierarchical relationship which detracts from an exploration of the patient's mental state. Thus, maintaining an open stance is not simply a matter of saying the proper things. There can be no script and there are many helpful things to say, any of which may be appropriate. It is a matter of being present and trying to understand. Some of the characteristics which will help therapists to avoid these pitfalls include a level of comfort with vulnerability and contradiction, a willingness to abandon the need for premature certainty or control over patients, and engagement in a process of continuous self-reflection.

Consider the patient who says he comes to session to appease his persecutors. Any number of responses are possible from an open stance including noticing that the persecutory belief is all-consuming and leaves no room for other ideas or that the therapist feels she will offend the patient if she is not alarmed by the patient's message. Alternately, a therapist might say: "So we may be stuck here. You seem to be sure that talking to me will ward off the people who want to kill you, but I have no knowledge about any people like that." Or similarly: "This is a tough spot. I know you don't want me to be against you, but it seems you can't help but be convinced that I'm conspiring against you. But I am stuck since I know that I am not. So it could be a pretty quiet hour today." These comments are considered to be grounded in an open stance because they are offered in the interest of understanding and not in getting the patient to do something.

Importantly, assuming an open stance does not require therapists to abandon their psychological expertise or any other potentially valuable knowledge. There is no reason to think that sharing expertise will disrupt dialogue when it is shared with the intent of mutual understanding. However, as May (1958) writes, "the therapist is assumedly an expert but if he is not first of all a human his expertness will be irrelevant and quite possibly harmful" (p. 82). As a result, even as the therapist has a fallible subjectivity, it is also a subjectivity that may come with potentially meaningful knowledge.

A final key point is that this process of sharing thoughts and ideas is likely to be distressing to many patients. The disturbances in the sense of self that accompany schizophrenia can make the process of being understood by another person especially difficult and overwhelming (Lysaker & Lysaker, 2010). If it is difficult to form complex ideas of ourselves, it may be threatening to encounter others who are able to understand us in a way we cannot, leading to feelings of helplessness or confusion. Similarly, since metacognitive deficits may leave persons with schizophrenia vulnerable to losing their sense of self in the face of the therapist's thoughts, they may feel "engulfed" by this close contact with others, as Laing (1978) and other existential psychiatrists have described. It may also be overwhelming to the patient that the clinician has specific ideas about her and expresses them. This is not to say that the patient should be seen as fragile, but it is important for therapists to be aware of the potential for these difficulties to arise and then name and discuss them if they do.

Struggles with intersubjectivity call for patience, respect, and reflection. It can also be important that what therapists share be clearly demarcated as something from their mind, not a statement about reality. For example, therapists can preface their comments with statements like: "What you are saying makes me have the thought that . . ." Other verbalizations that can accomplish this include: "As I listen to you, I'm forming the picture that . . ." or "As you are talking I am having an idea; should I share that now or do you want me to hold on to it for later?" This tempers the reflection and makes it clear that it is a piece of the therapist's experience that is being shared which can be reflected upon. Additionally, if patients clearly say they do not want to know the therapist's thoughts, these comments implicitly establish that the therapist is having thoughts, albeit unwanted, that could potentially be accessed later or even shared again if appropriate. For instance, if the patient says she does not want to hear the therapist's thoughts because they do not matter to her, it could be considered at that point (or later) whether there are perhaps some conditions under which those thoughts might matter (e.g., if they praised or supported the patient).

Since it is inevitable that therapists will share thoughts that are disturbing to patients, Table 7.1 offers examples of verbalizations which insert the therapist's mind in a manner that sustains dialogue. This can often be accomplished by asking patients what it was like to hear the therapist's thoughts.

Table 7.1 Interventions to Sustain Dialogue

After a specific therapist comment has disturbed dialogue

- I think I have said something that has upset your thinking.
- My idea seems to have upset you.
- As I shared my thought it seems like our conversation was interrupted.

Anticipating any comment or insertion of the therapist's mind will disturb dialogue

- I have the feeling it is hard to be sitting here with me.
- When I speak I think it upsets your thinking.
- I wonder if you want my mind far away.
- My ideas are certainly an interruption today.

Anticipating a specific comment will disturb dialogue

- I notice you are (doing a certain thing), and I am wondering if you would prefer I not notice or comment upon that.
- I notice we are not talking about (something obvious), and I am wondering if I should ask about it, or would you rather I ignore it?
- I have a different idea about what you are saying but am not sure if you want that kind of thought right now.
- I see you have a certain (facial expression or bodily posture), and I am wondering if I can ask about it.
- You haven't mentioned (a certain past topic) and it keeps coming up in my mind, but I'm not sure if you would like me to bring it up.

Patient responses can include any of a range of contradictory and complementary responses including feeling reassured, threatened, angered, challenged, affirmed, or belittled. This can also allow patients to notice at an elemental level what it is like for another person to think about them and provides a wide range of in-the-moment experiences which can become the subject of reflection and integration.

MERIT-TAS Element 2

The MERIT Therapist Adherence Scale (MERIT-TAS) Element 2 scale can be found in Table 7.2 As noted in the table, satisfactory adherence to this element requires frequent attempts by the therapist to insert their mind in a manner that does not derail dialogue. Optimal levels of adherence require not only frequent attempts to insert the therapist's mind but discussion of the patient's experience of the therapist's thoughts.

Table 7.2 MERIT-TAS Element 2 Scale

Score	*Level of Adherence*	*Therapist Behavior*
0	Absent	Failure to insert the therapist's mind
1	Marginal	Singular or infrequent attempts to insert the therapist's mind
2	Satisfactory	Frequent attempts across the course of the session to insert the therapist's mind in a manner that does not derail dialogue
3	Optimal	Frequent attempts to insert the therapist's mind in a manner that does not derail dialogue **and** reflection upon the impact of the therapist's mind on the patient

8 Element 3

Eliciting the Narrative Episode

The third element involves attending to and reflecting with patients about how they narrate their own stories and describe how they think about themselves. While the first two elements foster awareness of patients' experiences of their own mental states in the moment, this element expands this process and asks the therapist to think with patients about their experience in specific and personal terms about the events in their lives. MERIT refers to those specific experiences and events as narrative episodes.

The creation and consideration of narrative episodes is a common human activity. Individual stories provide many of the important pieces that are essential for people to authentically know another. It is within our unique narrative that we access and form ideas about ourselves so they can be shared with others and ultimately adapted and revised in the face of continued participation in the world.

MERIT emphasizes narratives because we believe that any attempt to understand the unique experience of another is most likely to produce genuine awareness when the objects of reflection are specific and detailed autobiographical episodes (Dimaggio et al., 2007, 2012, 2015). We agree with Fonagy et al. (2011, p. 104) who write how "a focus on episodic memory is the most productive material to use in elaborating the patient's self-understanding and understanding of others."

Eliciting and exploring a narrative is not the same as collecting a psychosocial history. The therapist's goal is not to gather the most accurate or objective account of a set of circumstances nor is the role one of historian, detective, or journalist. Rather, the therapist is seeking to form a joint understanding of the patient's thoughts, feelings, and intentions as they have emerged in unique contexts within a unique life so that a richer, more integrated understanding of the patient can emerge and be the basis for helping him to clarify and move toward his goals in recovery.

Further, narratives not only supply details to be potentially integrated but also provide the context for understanding any current set of events. A complexly integrated idea of a given patient may be incomplete if it does not include things such as his childhood living arrangements, attachments to family and peers, early experiences with sexuality, trauma, and simple daily experiences. Narratives not only supply details to be potentially integrated but also provide the context for understanding any current set of events. The meaning of any particular loss or struggle in the moment is only intelligible if enough of the history that surrounds it is known.

The kinds of narrative episodes produced will often evolve over the course of treatment. Early in therapy, patients may offer a narrative episode of an event that is rather skeletal. Over time, patients may return to the same episode again and again, describing it with richer detail and clarity, particularly once the patient has established gains in metacognitive capacity. In time, patients may be able to link narrative episodes from different sessions to one another and begin to recognize patterns across their lifetime. In this way, patients become able to produce narratives that evolve in complexity with telling and retelling.

Eliciting and Exploring Narratives

Narratives sometimes emerge in sessions spontaneously. For example, the patient may simply share a narrative episode without prompting and mention an event that happened recently or about which he has been thinking. The dyad then begins to think about and explore that narrative, elucidating its details. Since almost every narrative is composed of innumerable elements that can be explored, quite a bit of material is potentially available. Consider the patient who reports sitting in a movie theater for 20 minutes and then realizing he was not watching the movie he intended to see. Beyond the sequence of event reporting, we can imagine the patient traveling to the movie theater, planning to see a movie, sitting in the theater, and then realizing his error. However, there were also events that preceded and followed this. Certain things led to the decision to see this specific movie at this specific theater at this specific time. What was the cue that told the patient this was the wrong movie? What did he do after learning this, and what was his response, even later that day? There are also generally people involved in narrative episodes. Who were the people physically present, what were they thinking, and what might they have said later? What did the patient notice and not notice about those others? What mental activity was the patient aware of that occurred in his own mind during this event? How was it alike and different from other recent events in the mind of the patient?

Since the therapist could explore any number of these avenues, it is helpful for the clinician's queries to proceed from the picture she is forming about the events, noticing what is missing or seemingly contradictory as well how it fits with the patient's past experiences. Patients can become quickly overwhelmed if too many details are requested or the therapist fires questions one after another. As a result, a narrative episode should be examined in a manner that will best facilitate the process of joint exploration.

The type of questions asked need to be based on the degree of trust established with the patient, his background and history, as well as verbal and non-verbal behavior in the session. Therapists may have a preferred style of seeking information but still must be thinking in the moment and not referring to a formula or going on "auto pilot" when seeking to understand the patient. Finally, exploring a narrative will often reveal surprising information that will open new avenues for exploration. For instance, if the patient reveals he went to the movie to avoid a drug dealer, had just hung up on his brother who was admonishing him, or went to that specific theater hoping to strike up a conversation with the ticket taker whom he had seen there previously, the therapist might form a different idea leading to new things about which to be curious and inquire.

The therapist's goal is to understand, and the exploration of a narrative episode should not unfold into an interrogation or search for a disembodied truth. The optimal outcome is a shared richer understanding of a patient's experience. In our example, the therapist's inquiries might lead to a shared picture of the patient as a dissociated observer of the world who has little sense that he can find a way to meet his needs or perhaps even name them. Alternatively, themes of the patient desperately trying to avoid drugs or feeling inadequate compared to his sibling could emerge as illuminated by the narrative. If the patient does not spontaneously share related narrative episodes, the therapist can simply ask if the patient can think of a similar or contrasting event and then continue exploration of the new narrative.

In our example of the patient who inadvertently went to the wrong theater, the therapist might ask about similar or contrasting narratives and elicit stories about a time in the military when he felt a deep loneliness and confusion or a time during a marriage when he felt competent and connected to others. Alternatively, a patient might describe a time when he was free of drugs during his first marriage but is now in the grip of addiction. The patient might also describe a time in high school when he felt could do anything as well as his siblings or an event in early adulthood when he was able to help a sibling in trouble. Regardless of the content, the therapist and patient should explore the new narrative episode with the goal of developing a richer sense of the patient as a unique person which could again lead to yet another narrative episode.

Assisting Patients to Engage in the Narrative Process

Not all sessions will flow smoothly. There will be times when patients do not spontaneously relate a narrative episode or offer only abstractions such as "I am anxious," "I am tired," or "I am the kind of person who gives too much."

Patients may also say they have nothing to say or offer a story that is not intended as a subject for reflection but to illustrate a point such as how cold their partner is, that they are blameless in a conflict, or how cleverly they managed a cantankerous family member.

In these cases, the therapist should nevertheless try to elicit a narrative. For the patient who offers only an abstract description of herself, the therapist can ask about a specific time and place where that abstraction held true. For example, if a patient says she is just angry, the therapist might ask things such as: "Can you tell me about another time this week when you were angry?" or "What was happening during that time to make you angry?" or "Who else was around?" or "Did those other people know you were angry?" or "Can you tell me about a time recently when you felt differently?"

For the patient who says she has nothing to offer, therapists can simply ask about the patient and her life. Based upon his knowledge of the patient's life and level of trust that has been established, the therapist can inquire about her past such as where the patient was born or went to school or events as recent as those that took place right before the patient came to session. For example, "What happened when you traveled to session today?"

In the face of a narrative which is being offered only to establish a point (e.g., the coldness of a partner), the therapist can identify this as part of the patient's agenda and then ask about the events prior to and following the event, and other similar and dissimilar events. For instance, if a patient appears to be attempting to establish that his partner is unfaithful, the therapist might ask if and when the patient has had similar experiences with other people. Alternately, if it becomes apparent that the patient is overly concerned with a partner whom she fears will abandon her, the therapist might ask about how the patient's last relationship started and ended.

In each of these cases, the optimal outcome is a richer understanding of patients as illuminated by the events in their lives leading to even more narrative episodes. The types of narratives that are developed should be based on the therapist's intuitions about the kinds of stories that will be relevant in the context of the patient's background. Prompting for narratives which may expose patients' emotional vulnerabilities should be done in a way that will ultimately lead to the patient's psychic growth and take into account the current level of trust in the therapy relationship.

While we have focused on direct inquiry to explore and elicit narratives, there are other means as well. In our experience, therapist disclosure can be useful for some patients in bringing up new narratives. For example, disclosure can provide an example of how to tell a story or also make the patient feel safer and more connected to the therapist. Indeed, some patients will solicit such disclosures. For instance, a patient told a story of bullying someone when he was young and asked if the therapist had ever treated people cruelly when he was young. The therapist related a story of having done so which led the patient to reflect both on his own narrative and then to produce others. Another patient faltered in discussing a poignant feeling of abandonment by a partner. The therapist then shared a story of rejection from his past which spurred the patient to expand his own narrative and relate it to others. That being said, self-disclosure needs to be used appropriately and should be avoided if it serves the function of meeting a therapist's own need to feel understood. Additionally, we have found that patient photo albums or diary entries can also be useful in generating narratives for some patients but obviously only if the patient wants to share them.

Barriers to Obtaining a Narrative

Several issues often surface when eliciting narratives in treatment sessions. Patients may be unaccustomed to talking about their lives or even being asked about them. Others may not feel worthy of telling their life story and wonder, "Why are you asking me?" or "How is this relevant?" In response, a therapist may explain that a story illustrating what the patient has shared will help the therapist and patient to jointly understand the patient's unique experience. Therapists might also need to share how the meaning of an event depends upon its context within the patient's life. For example, the meaning of a college degree would differ depending upon whether the person had a long history of academic achievement or struggled throughout her school career. That degree would also take on a different meaning if the patient were the only person in her family to have completed college or if, by contrast, everyone else had already earned graduate degrees. Similarly, the breakup of a relationship would have different meaning if it were the only romantic relationship the patient had experienced or if it lacked the intensity and commitment of previous relationships.

Other patients may have basic dialogical or cognitive disturbances that make it difficult for them to produce a narrative with much complexity or to see how one narrative may be related to another. If asked to think of an experience or story that is similar to one that they just reported (e.g., finding themselves in the wrong movie theater), they may sit silently in confusion or offer something that is delusional or disorganized. In such cases, therapists should accept whatever the patient can provide or perhaps simply may ask for more details about something the patient had commented on previously. For even the most barren or cacophonous patients, a narrative episode can often be constructed by concretely detailing the events that took place from the time they awoke to how they now find themselves in the office. These patients also were born in particular places so it may be possible to form brief narratives and think about experiences living in different settings. Therapists can be creative in responding to these dilemmas as well. In the past, we have looked at online maps of places where patients lived which assisted them to talk about an event that took place at those locations, including routes walked to work, street corners where drugs could be readily obtained, and places where a high school prom was held.

Difficulties producing narrative episodes may also reflect a lack of trust or a recent rupture in the relationship. These circumstances may necessitate time and patience for trust to develop or perhaps an intervention to repair the relationship before narrative episodes will emerge. It may also be difficult for patients to produce a narrative episode after a traumatic experience has left them in an emotionally dysregulated state and needing to feel more emotionally settled before a narrative episode can be produced.

Other patients may offer narratives that contain material which seems to be untrue or manifestly delusional. This could include content in which the patient's accomplishments or the misdeeds of others range from potentially exaggerated to highly improbable. For example, a seemingly unathletic patient might report he was a star high school athlete or played minor league baseball. Another patient with a history of poor academic achievement and unemployment might describe being a successful banker, an arms trader in Asia, or commissioner of the National Basketball Association.

In these situations, while therapists should not play detective and try to catch the patient in a lie or become consumed with checking every detail hoping to confirm inaccuracies, they should also not deny their sense that something may be inaccurate or inauthentic. Certainly, a story that seems improbable may be true. The patient who says he was an informant for the FBI may turn out to have been one. What therapists should not do is pursue details about a narrative they believe to be basically untrue because that would be inauthentic and work against MERIT's basic principles. Rather, therapists should look for elements of the narrative they believe to be veridical and use that as a basis for querying about the patient's life. For example, if a patient says she was in prison with Albert Einstein, and it is known that she was previously incarcerated, details about prison life might be elicited and explored as well as material about her life before and after prison.

Finally, there are also things that clinicians may do that impair the process of narrative generation. One pitfall is for therapists to believe they "already know the story" and miss opportunities to learn new details and gain a richer picture that can be mutually understood by the dyad. Many narratives will be appropriate to revisit repeatedly. Failures to understand cultural differences or assumptions of cultural homogeneity can also become barriers to mutual reflection. Finally, attending to the mundane problems that frequently emerge in some patients' lives can lead therapists away from thinking about the larger picture of the patient's life and lose the narrative focus.

MERIT-TAS Element 3

MERIT Therapist Adherence Scale (MERIT-TAS) Element 3 scale can be found in Table 8.1. Satisfactory adherence to this element requires frequent attempts by the therapist to elicit narrative episodes or the emergence and joint discussion of a narrative episode. Optimal levels of adherence require the emergence and discussion about a narrative episode and nuanced and significant exploration of the details of that narrative episode.

Table 8.1 MERIT-TAS Element 3 Scale

Score	*Level of Adherence*	*Therapist Behavior*
0	Absent	Failure to attempt to elicit narrative episode or the lack of the emergence of a substantial narrative episode
1	Marginal	Singular or infrequent attempts to elicit a narrative episode without the emergence of a substantial narrative episode
2	Satisfactory	Frequent attempts across the course of the session to elicit a narrative episode or the emergence of a substantial narrative episode
3	Optimal	The emergence of a substantial narrative episode with nuanced exploration of relevant details

9 Element 4

Defining the Psychological Problem

Element 4 asks the therapist to jointly identify and reflect with a patient upon a plausible psychological problem she is currently facing. Here, the therapist and patient should be thinking together about the psychological difficulties that the patient experiences. A problem is something that frustrates a goal, need, wish, or desire. It must also be a psychological problem that is plausible. As a result, hallucinations or unlikely beliefs are not usually psychological problems, but the feelings of loneliness that result from being shunned as a "voice hearer" or as a person with eccentric beliefs are. As with the preceding elements, this does not necessitate agreement about the "correct" or "true" problem but rather conjoint reflection upon it. Since the goal of this process is to isolate a psychological challenge which can then be a topic of joint reflection by the patient and therapist, it should not be reduced to the idea that the therapist should "get" the patient to take responsibility.

Problems will span a wide range of issues. They may be something anticipated, currently experienced, or represent a loss. For example, feelings of affiliation and safety may be threatened by the declining health of a parent, a new demand in a relationship, or the death of a loved one. Similarly, they may be in response to either an acute development (e.g., loneliness due to a recent move to an unfamiliar part of town) or a long-standing issue the patient has grappled with for years (e.g., chronic feelings of social isolation).

The distress associated with the problem may be expressed in a variety of ways including acute discomfort, a vague sense of being ill at ease, numbness, a lack of a sense of meaning, or emptiness. Patients may also experience anhedonia or feel unable to manage their own emotions. There will be times when emotional states are closely tied to very specific events or people and others where they will be highly diffuse and associated with virtually everything. Distress may also be bound up in bodily states and covertly expressed as "something is wrong with my heart," or "I know I have cancer."

Defining the Problem

This element calls for joint consideration about how the patient is facing a recognizable challenge and has a recognizable response to it. However, awareness of a mental illness or having insight is not necessarily a precondition (e.g., a patient can deny she is ill and not see any consequences of a mental illness in her life yet still feel unable to manage her emotions). Consequently, the psychological problem does not have to be connected to a diagnostic label, identification of symptoms, or framed as a skill deficit.

As a result, a diagnosis of schizophrenia, a hallucination, or not knowing how to approach a potential romantic interest are not psychological problems in and of themselves. However, feeling ostracized by family due to a mental health diagnosis, being unable to connect to others because of continuous hallucinations, or feeling isolated due to a lack of a partner are psychological problems. Similarly, having poor coping skills is also not likely to be a psychological problem while feeling overwhelmed, confused, and flooded with awful feelings likely is. In our experience, psychological problems are rarely ever best expressed as a symptom. For example, the underlying problem faced by the patient with severe paranoia is often not so much global suspiciousness, but a deep sense of worry, insecurity, isolation, and anger.

In summary, this element asks the therapist to help the patient to find a plausible problem upon which they both agree. As with the agenda, patients are likely to have multiple psychological problems that vary in terms of integration and degree of immediate awareness. The essential clinical task, then, is for the dyad to think together about the problem and make the patient's experience of it available for exploration and integration.

How Problems Emerge in Sessions

The initial discovery of the psychological problem can be made entirely by the patient or the therapist. The patient may clearly articulate it or the therapist may recognize it in what the patient is saying or in her nonverbal behavior. Frequently, psychological problems will emerge as patients recount narrative episodes. From the specifics of the story, a sense of the patient as a protagonist facing identifiable dilemmas may develop and become the subject of joint reflection. To detect the psychological problem within a narrative episode, the therapist needs to engage in dialogue with the patient to develop a picture of the actual events which were related to the perceived frustration of the patient's relevant goal, need, wish, or desire.

Consider the previous patient who tells the story of fleeing a church meeting. In response to the therapist asking the patient to share what happened prior to and following the moment he left, the patient revealed that he had been planning to attend this event for a long time and had some comments he wanted to share. However, he forgot them in his anxiety and then imagined others staring at him critically, leading him to rush from the room and stand outside in front of the church.

At this point, the patient and therapist might shift to thinking about the larger gestalt of the story and, specifically, which of the patient's needs were being frustrated or blocked. What are the barriers faced by the patient and what is their effect? What are the consequent changes in the patient's mind? Based upon discussion, the following problem might be discovered: the patient came to the meeting with a desire for affiliation and affirmation of his standing in the community but felt this was threatened, leading to distress and his leaving precipitously with hopes that others would follow and soothe him. If pursued further, the discussion might also lead to the recognition of an even larger problem: the patient's struggles with a pervasive sense of personal inadequacy and failure in multiple social roles.

As a second illustration, consider a patient who commented that something about the last few days had been difficult but she was unable to quite say why. To understand this, the therapist tried to elicit a narrative episode by asking when this had occurred. In response, the patient appeared confused but after noting that the current day was Monday, she said she was talking about Sunday. The therapist tried to elicit an elaboration and the patient told the story of how over the weekend, she made a trip to the corner grocery store after realizing there was no food in her apartment. While shopping, she encountered no one she knew and returned home. Once alone in her apartment, she experienced terrible stomach pain which she decided meant she was suffering from cancer. To understand the psychological problem, the therapist tried to explore how this was threatening which led to the joint conclusion that the patient had felt her life was threatened and there was no one who might help. This led to their agreeing that the patient's psychological problem was feeling alone and vulnerable.

Common Challenges in Defining Problems

Constructing a psychological problem from a narrative may be challenging for patients who concretely assert that their problem is the frustration of need alone (e.g., their problem is a lack of housing or a sibling's anger). In responding to these concrete stances, the distress should be affirmed but the focus directed to the patient's psychological processes. Therapists might say: "I'm thinking it must be hard to feel good about yourself when you don't have a place to live" or "Seeing your sister angry, I would guess, causes emotions you can't quiet." Responses of this nature can serve to effectively refocus joint reflection back on the mental life of the patient and elicit an account of psychological processes.

As might be anticipated, persons with limited metacognitive capacity may have difficulties naming psychological processes so their exploration may call for the use of highly simplified and non-complex language that simply locates a gross disturbance within the patient. However, even in the absence of a narrative episode, the joint identification of the patient's immediate goals and desires may point to a potential psychological problem. In these situations, the therapist should form an idea of what psychological problem might fuel the patient's current behavior and directly inquire about it in language that the patient will understand. If the patient is in a deeply paranoid state, the therapist might hypothesize that this is an expression of intense fear of being criticized. Here, the therapist might say something like: "More than anything today you have to protect whatever shreds of dignity you have to keep people from destroying it."

Consider the clinician who conjectures that the patient finds the experience of the therapist sharing her mind to be intimidating and being around others seems like an imminent threat to the his sense of basic identity. Here, the clinician might say: "Right now, everything is too much and you have to keep it away so you won't disappear." Similarly, for the seemingly barren or empty patient, the problem could be that the patient can find no thoughts at the moment and may desperately want to escape the session. Here, the therapist might merely state this and wonder if the patient would agree or disagree, taking care not to overwhelm or pressure the patient into agreeing.

When the psychological problem is detected from the agenda or reaction to the therapist, this may then lead to the elicitation of a narrative episode to better understand the nature of the problem. However, while we have separated the narrative episode and psychological problem for purposes of discussion, it may be difficult to know exactly when the sharing of a narrative episode is complete and it is time to define the problem. It is not uncommon for psychological problems and narratives to feed into one another in an iterative process.

MERIT's emphasis on understanding the psychological problem within the moment or a narrative episode diverges from other approaches that do not rely as heavily on the linkage to a specific memory or experience. Explicitly, we favor focusing on narrative episodes since this is how people construct meaning from their experience. When we revisit events in our lives, we recount them as they occurred over time. However, this process of retelling also provides the opportunity to form new ideas about what occurred, the challenges we have encountered, and ultimately our sense of ourselves. In this way, stories can provide the context for deciding what the past has meant and how we will choose to respond in the future.

This leads us to favor a less structured approach to obtaining narratives and often to ask people what memories come to mind in the context of describing the challenges of their daily life. In contrast, more structured activities, such as role play, run the risk of bringing something to mind that was not in memory. While such techniques are not necessarily without value, the more the psychological problem under consideration is shaped and influenced by the therapist, the more it is an abstraction and less a recognizable part of one's unique experience of life.

The Importance of Authenticity

As essential as anything else in this process, the psychological problem must be a matter that is mutually agreed upon in the moment. Whether the patient states that she is struggling with something or the therapist infers as much from her speech and non-verbal behavior, it must make sense to both the patient and therapist. As a result, there are times when the question of authenticity needs to be considered.

We find there are four common barriers to authenticity in this process. First, *the threat described by the patient may appear implausible.* For example, a patient may find that his fame as a world renowned religious figure frustrates his ability to think about other things such as forming a romantic attachment. Another patient may state that the messages a political figure is sending him through the television are degrading his self-esteem. In these cases, while the therapists can empathize with the authentic unmet needs, they cannot authentically join in reflecting upon what caused the dilemma. Alternately, there are other cases when a *patient expresses recognizable threats to needs linked with emotional states with which the therapist cannot genuinely empathize.* For example, a patient may say a date left him alone in a restaurant which affirmed his desire to run for president.

In both of these situations, the therapist should focus on what he does understand and believe and avoid aligning himself with what he does not. In the first example, the therapist might reflect jointly on the problem of not having a partner or in the second acknowledge that being left alone in a public place could create a negative response. If judged clinically appropriate, clinicians might also self-disclose having had similar unmet needs or facing similarly distressing situations. Here, just as self-disclosure may scaffold the construction of narrative episodes, it may also scaffold the elucidation of psychological problems.

A third threat to the authenticity occurs when the *patient is unable to identify any distress whatsoever* (e.g., only expresses a grandiose oneness with the world or a solipsistic joy in holding a deeply idiosyncratic belief). Here, the agenda may be a clear: to share that joy or bliss replete with narrative episodes about ministering to others. In these cases, the therapist may be able to do little more than state the patient does not seem to experience any problems whatsoever at present. Such a statement may contain the kernel of a problem, namely the patient is unable to notice something everyone experiences. As a result, a psychological problem can sometimes be found in the reluctance to find a psychological problem. Again, it may be helpful for therapists to self-disclose something minor they are currently confronting in the hopes of scaffolding the patient's construction of a problem in the moment. Alternately, if the therapist's inability to understand these states frustrates the patient, this too might be identified as a psychological problem. Here, therapists can say: "You're filled with this experience and it is maddening that I cannot understand," or "My slowness to get you today is a problem."

A fourth difficulty emerges when *patients present material which takes the form of a psychological problem but is not.* For example, a patient might report violent command hallucinations or thoughts of suicide in order to provoke the therapist to panic. There may be many dynamics underlying this including a wish to mobilize the therapist and create tension in her which reduces the tension experienced by the patient. Inauthentic problems can also be presented to distract the therapist and patient alike from discussing something distressing. For instance, a patient might report heightened anxiety so that the patient's continued substance use remains outside of consideration. It may also be that the patient thinks she is fulfilling her role as a good patient when she says she is lonely or stigmatized at her job by quickly producing a psychological problem that may not be a significant issue for her in reality. Additionally, a "false" psychological problem might also be offered because the patient thinks it is what the therapist wants or fears that the "real" psychological problem would overwhelm the clinician.

As in daily life, there is not a failsafe way to detect when inauthenticity is present. To make these judgments, therapists must use their intuition which can sometimes be informed by the close monitoring of their own internal states. Hints that this is happening might be found in an uncharacteristic failure on the part of the therapist to feel empathy in response to a purported dilemma that would typically elicit his empathy. Lack of congruence between the patient's report and appearance as well as contradictions within narrative episodes may also suggest that what is being presented is only masquerading as a psychological problem. For example, the patient who is sharing problems because he thinks that is his job may appear pleased when he can carefully describe them but has little interest in actually exploring them in detail since their report was really the goal. Again, intuition may be required to decide when patients are presenting something to cater to what they believe the therapist wants to hear or can tolerate.

Inauthentic problems should not be necessarily discarded but seen as having potential meaning, including possibly pointing to a new agenda. For instance, the patient who is supplying non-existent problems might be helped to see one of his agendas is to play the "perfect patient." Similarly, if it appears that an aspect of an agenda is to protect the therapist, the clinician might express gratitude for the patient's concern while also reassuring her that he will not be harmed by anything she reveals.

Evolution of Psychological Problems Over the Course of Treatment

The psychological problems discovered in the agenda or a narrative episode may be something that was previously identified or the further elaboration of an older problem. Alternately, it could be something entirely new and never have been discussed previously. Regardless, while the psychological problem need not necessarily be linked with previous problems, it is likely that as patients begin to integrate information more and more deeply over time, themes will emerge. For example, discussions about difficulties in multiple relationships may come to share the common thread of feeling unlovable or having no real qualities which others might treasure. Consequently, as psychotherapy unfolds, therapists should wonder whether the psychological problems of the session have elements in common with previous psychological problems. And if so, therapists should wonder to what extent the psychological problem is a natural outgrowth of previous problems or other problems.

As with all matters in MERIT, how problems might be linked should be the subject of joint discussion. While patients may not have answers to all or even any of these possibilities, asking these questions is critical. First, it may help evolve a more nuanced picture of the psychological problem the patient is facing. Second, it may offer an opportunity for patients to not only identify something they struggle with but also to frame the psychological problem as a subject of reflection itself, that is, as something to be considered outside of seeking a solution.

Pursuing these avenues of inquiry position patients as reflective agents and avoids a possible rush to find an answer which may prematurely foreclose reflectivity. Of course, comparing psychological problems to previous problems may not be possible early in therapy because there is little shared history in the relationship. There may also be times when comparing a psychological problem to others interrupts the flow of thought and should be avoided. Further, as when Elements 7 and 8 are discussed, reflection about psychological challenges should be presented at metacognitive levels that allow the patient to understand them.

MERIT-TAS Element 4

MERIT Therapist Adherence Scale (MERIT-TAS) Element 4 scale can be found in Table 9.1. As noted in the table, satisfactory adherence to this element requires either multiple attempts across different part of the course of the session

Table 9.1 MERIT-TAS Element 4 Scale

Score	*Level of Adherence*	*Therapist Behavior*
0	Absent	Failure to attempt to elicit a psychological problem or lack of the emergence of a substantial psychological problem
1	Marginal	Singular or infrequent attempts to elicit a psychological problem without the emergence of a substantial psychological problem
2	Satisfactory	Frequent attempts across the course of the session to elicit a psychological problem **or** the emergence of a substantial psychological problem
3	Optimal	The emergence of a substantial psychological problem with nuanced discussion of its connection with other problems or aspects of the patient's life

by therapists to elicit a psychological problem *or* the emergence within session of a substantial psychological problem. An optimal level of adherence requires both the emergence of a psychological problem and a nuanced discussion of that problem linking it with other challenges the patient has faced or other parts of the patient's life.

Recapitulation of Chapters 6 Through 9

To this point, we have reviewed MERIT's four content elements: seeking the agenda, asking the therapist to form and share thoughts with the patient in a manner that promotes dialogue, focusing on narratives, and reflecting with patients on the challenges that they face. Each of these elements offers increasingly diverse material which can be integrated into the kinds of complex ideas about self and others needed for patients to direct their own recovery. Considering each of these four content elements will lead to the development of an increasing number of ideas about patients' intentions, their reactions to others' awareness of them, the events of their lives, and their larger struggles. However, therapists also need to be aware that discomfort with vulnerability and uncertainty, taking matters at face value, being unwilling to see the deeper and more complex sides of patients, or feeling a need to control patients will quickly undermine any efforts to use these elements effectively.

As discussed earlier, MERIT's elements are not expected to flow or emerge in a certain order. Rather, a synergy will often emerge. Successfully finding an agenda opens the possibility for therapists to insert their own mind, find narrative episodes, and explore psychological problems. Successfully inserting one's mind opens doors to finding new patient agendas, narrative episodes, and psychological problems. Successfully pursuing a narrative episode opens the possibility for therapists to find new agendas, to insert their own mind, and to find psychological problems, while finding coherent psychological problems again opens the door for further work on the three other elements.

10 Element 5

Reflecting on the Therapeutic Relationship

In its first four elements, MERIT focuses on patients' sense of themselves and others as they become apparent in the agenda, reactions to the therapist, personal narratives, and psychological problems. In Element 5, MERIT asks therapists to jointly reflect with patients about their relationship, the context in which all of these things are being explored. This explicitly makes the relationship itself the subject of reflection.

MERIT is based upon the premise that all metacognitive acts are by their nature intersubjective. Throughout life, when we think meaningfully about ourselves and others, it is always in the context of relationships. Often, we realize something about ourselves or others after sharing our thoughts with someone else (e.g., a lover, religious leader, teacher, colleague, fellow student). Even when we are alone, there is always a possible addressee of our thoughts. For instance, when driving alone, thoughts that emerge about the meaning of something you or another person did always have an imagined audience. We have a sense that the things we or someone else did might be judged differently by different people. We can imagine who might find our thoughts meaningful and who would be confused by them. This imaginary commentator might also include people who are deceased or no longer part of our lives such as a beloved teacher or an estranged parent.

The essential component of Element 5 is that there be joint reflection about the interpersonal processes that are occurring in the therapist-patient dyad. As with the other elements, there is not a mandated set of questions or specific amount of time and attention directed to discussing the relationship. What is critical, though, is that metacognitive activity about the relationship be facilitated.

Critical Components of the Therapeutic Relationship

In MERIT, the therapist's role refers to how the patient perceives the therapist and the qualities seen in the therapist as he is listening to and thinking with her. As might be expected, the full range of identifiable dimensions of the therapist's role is potentially very broad and can include a myriad of personal characteristics and requirements that can shift over time and may contain complementary, contradictory, and unrelated ideas.

This element requires therapists to flexibly think with patients about their experience of the relationship and encourage patients to use the words that best describe it. This process also requires therapists to communicate to patients that they have full permission to share negative as well as positive thoughts, which is sometimes a daunting task given the power differential in the relationship. MERIT also holds that a meaningful reflection can take place even if there are episodic negative aspects to the therapeutic relationship, and progress is not necessarily dependent upon a maintaining an unfailingly positive tone. While a positively valenced relationship may have its advantages, persons with serious mental illness, as is true for everyone, can still make meaning within relationships that have challenging aspects. A technical point is that patients may also need reassurance that they can raise aspects of their experience which may not be considered to be acceptable topics in everyday conversation. For example, this might include noticing that the therapist is obese, seems angry and punitive, is advanced in years, seems too young, or is sexually attractive.

How the Therapy Relationship Supports Metacognitive Activity

There are four major aspects of the therapeutic relationship that support metacognitive activity which require attention: the therapist's general role(s) as a partner in dialogue, the potential effect of that role on the wellness of the patient, how well the therapist is conforming to that role, and the patient's reaction to the therapist's performance of the role(s).

Perceptions of the Therapist's Role as a Partner in Dialogue

Discussions about the therapy relationship can be elicited by the therapist asking the patient how she sees him. Opportunities to ask about these perceptions may include instances when patients comment on the relationship or respond to the therapist in a way that is surprising, leading the therapist to wonder how he is being seen. Inquiries about patient perceptions may also be in order after something major has been established in treatment in order to see if the therapist is now somehow seen differently by the patient. Therapists should also use their own intuition to make guesses about how they are viewed. If therapists feel pressed to be doing a certain thing, they may ask in a neutral manner if that is their role. For example, if the therapist feels positioned to criticize the patient, to catch the patient moving to relapse, to encourage the patient to achieve something, or affirm the patient's basic worth, he can ask if that is his role. Similarly, if the therapist feels confused, he might choose to share this as well. When patients say they do not perceive the therapist as having any particular qualities or roles, this could itself be understood as a role.

There are times when the therapist's role is obvious and requires little comment. For instance, the patient who is describing a recent loss, placing the therapist in a role of intimate trust, most likely does not need to be asked to reflect about the therapist's role. Nevertheless, the therapist may note that his connection to the patient feels very intimate and privileged, allowing for the relationship to be a subject for reflection.

Therapists need to be aware that some patients will be able to offer only very vague descriptions of the therapeutic relationship while others may provide complex accounts, sometimes in surprising contrast with the patient's apparent intellectual or verbal abilities. The therapist's role may be viewed in some dyads as being similar to one of other specific people who have played a significant role in the patient's life such as a teacher, caretaker, younger brother, niece, religious advisor, friend, aunt, babysitter, coach, dean, probation officer, or partner. In others, it may be one that represents a puzzling interpersonal novelty and quite unlike what the patient has experienced in the past.

The role can also take on a more general character such as cheerleader, judge, someone in an enviable social position, a powerful authority figure who can authorize risk-taking, or one whose job it is to remain optimistic no matter what. Highly stigmatized patients may also expect the therapist to be the representative of the mental health field or someone who has made decisions for them in the past. Therapists can also find themselves in any number of different positions at different times. For instance, a patient discussing a conflict with a partner for which she did not want to feel responsible might see the therapist as a kind of doting uncle, a critical probation officer, a judgmental partner, and an attentive niece, all at different times. What remains essential is that the dyad thinks about these matters in an ongoing manner. As with other MERIT elements, the goal is not too get it "right" or to correct problems in the relationship. While the latter may be a side effect, the goal is for there to be joint reflection upon the relationship which establishes it as a subject for reflection.

Impact of the Therapist's Role Upon the Patient

Another issue to explore and discuss is whether the impact of the therapist's perceived role upon the patient is positive, negative, or both. While at times this will be obvious and not deserve comment (e.g., when an empathic role is successfully adopted by the therapist), there are others when the exploration will be revealing. For example, a patient may comment that he sees the therapist as an older person similar to her special education teacher who was a daily reminder that she was not as good as other people.

Exploration of a role might also reveal both its beneficial and problematic aspects. For instance, it may be helpful for the therapist to be seen in the role of a strict older figure because the patient has no faith in her ability to succeed and wants a trusted other to guide her in not sabotaging her efforts at becoming more active socially. On the other hand, this role may also serve to reinforce the patient's perceptions of her limitations and hinder her from learning to master her fears that she will be rejected in intimate social encounters.

This issue of whether a role is helpful to a patient may change from session to session. However, there are some roles, such as being seen as an adoring lover, that would almost never be helpful. A stalemate could emerge if the patient is convinced that the therapist should play a specific role and no other. In such a case, it might be discussed how there can only be one role and why playing any other one would be unacceptable. Given MERIT's focus on self-directed recovery, a helpful role is seen as one which promotes patients to think about their own thinking and to use that knowledge to address the difficulties they are facing.

Therapist Conformance With the Patient's Positioning

Another consideration may naturally arise: regardless of whether the therapist should play this role, how well is he playing it? For example, how well is the therapist doing as a non-judgmental observer or as an empathic source of support? If the therapist is jointly reflecting with the patient in the role of the judge, is he doing well at that or failing miserably in the patient's eyes? While discussing the potential impact of the therapist conforming to the role is not always a major consideration, it can serve to position the dyad to reflect upon what is happening with the behavior of the therapist being a subject for reflection. For example, it may be both important for the therapist to know if she was failing to appear empathic and validating for the patient to not only to be able to notice this but for her perception to be taken seriously. Such discussions also help to reinforce the perception of the relationship as being open, curious, and non-defensive.

Reactions to the Therapist's Role

A final aspect is concerned with the patient's *reaction to the therapist's performance* of the role, whether it be positive or negative. When therapists have identifiable roles, patients will naturally have reactions to them. For example, a patient may experience comfort in the therapist playing a role that is jointly understood as healthy, such as encouraging the patient to try to date or work. However, such responses need to be individualized because a deeply stigmatized patient or one who adapted to a sick role may be very uncomfortable with the therapist seeing his other aspects or encouraging him to take chances by doing things outside his comfort zone. In such a situation, it is not necessarily expected that the patient will endorse the therapist's not supporting the sick role, just recognition that this is what she is doing because the goal of this element is to promote joint understanding of the therapeutic relationship. Exploring these dynamics may also permit a more complete picture of what is happening in the relationship to emerge and be considered.

MERIT-TAS Element 5

MERIT Therapist Adherence Scale (MERIT-TAS) Element 5 scale can be found in Table 10.1. As noted in the table, satisfactory adherence to this element requires either frequent attempts to discuss the therapeutic relationship across the course of the session with consideration of the therapist's role or position or the emergence of a substantial statement about the therapeutic relationship. An optimal level of adherence requires the emergence of a substantial statement about the therapeutic relationship and a discussion of the meaning of that relationship including the role the therapist is positioned in and how helpful that role would or would not be.

Table 10.1 MERIT-TAS Element 5 Scale

Score	*Level of Adherence*	*Therapist Behavior*
0	Absent	Failure to discuss the therapeutic relationship
1	Marginal	Singular or infrequent attempts to discuss the therapeutic relationship with consideration of the therapist's role or position without the emergence of a substantial statement about the therapeutic relationship
2	Satisfactory	Frequent attempts to discuss the therapeutic relationship with consideration of the therapist's role or position or the emergence of a substantial statement about the therapeutic relationship
3	Optimal	The emergence of a substantial statement about the therapeutic relationship with consideration of the therapist's role or position **and** the usefulness of that position

11 Element 6

Reflecting on Progress

Element 6 is concerned with exploring patients' perceptions of how therapy is having an impact upon them. Stated otherwise, what has changed or is changing in the mind and life of the patient due to engaging in the activities described in the first five elements of MERIT? How do patients think about themselves or others differently? What are they able to do that they did not or could not do previously?

This element calls for another level of reflection in which there is joint consideration of what has taken place in therapy. This may center on a long-term goal or something that has just arisen in the session. It might also be seen in terms of specific outcomes (e.g., has the patient's level of distress improved, stayed the same, or worsened?) or unexpected or less concrete things (e.g., patient realizes that more is wrong in their life than they had previously been aware of or their life now feels generally less confusing more manageable). The intent of this element is to encourage therapists to stimulate patients' metacognition about the experience of therapy and see themselves as purposive beings who are in search of something.

In contrast with Element 5, this element is not concerned with how patients experience the therapist but how the session and treatment have affected the patient. As a result, a positive appraisal of the therapist may not always coincide with a positive appraisal of the effects of treatment. For instance, the patient may feel positively toward the therapist even though there has not been adequate progress. Conversely, the patient may feel like they are making progress but not necessarily feel positively about the therapist (e.g., as one might feel about a physical therapist). Additionally, while learning what patients think about progress may affect how future sessions are conducted, the purpose of this element is not to gather treatment planning information but to stimulate deeper reflection in the moment about the patient as an active agent whose thoughts, intentions, and feelings may change over time. In turn, this can be used as a subject for reflection as the patient becomes increasingly able to direct her own recovery.

Asking and Reflecting About Progress

The questions that the therapist might ask to stimulate thinking about progress should typically be simple as this is more likely to be effective than inquiries that are more complex. Examples include: "Is this helping?," "Are you getting what you hoped for?," "Was this worth your trip here?," "Are you glad you came in today?," or "What do you make of our visit today?"

Queries about progress should be framed neutrally unless the anticipated answer is fairly obvious based upon what is transpiring in the session. For example, if a patient appears either quite dissatisfied or satisfied, the therapist who asks neutrally about the effect of the session is liable to be experienced as being dismissive or disingenuous. A simple reflection such as "things are not going well today" might be needed and quite effective when a patient is clearly struggling. Similarly, if a session appeared manifestly successful it might be better to ask in question form "This seemed to go okay?" rather than making a neutral comment that might seem insensitive to something that was clearly important and helpful to the patient.

Responses to patients' appraisals should be simple as well. The goal is to think with patients about what they experience as a result of the session. Sometimes these responses will be sufficiently detailed that therapists feel they understand and nothing more needs to be said. Other times, though, the therapist may understand the patient's general experience but not why the patient had this experience. In that case, therapists should inquire about what made the session a positive or negative experience. If, for instance, the patient notes, "I feel better now," the therapist should ask, "How come?" and "In what way?" Was there something specific that was or was not helpful? Even if the session was generally helpful, it might be asked if there were parts that were more helpful than others. Does the patient have a personal interpretation or theory about why it is going well or not well? Previously, we noted that in gathering a narrative episode we were interested in facts, not theories. Here, we are looking for both details and abstractions as the patient steps back and considers what has happened in the session.

Querying About Change

A crucial aspect of this element concerns patients' perceptions of perceived changes (or lack thereof) in themselves and their lives. Was this something the patient had expected? Patients can be surprised, pleased, or displeased when the session results in a certain realization or change in their emotional state. They can also be surprised, pleased, or displeased when something does not change. Alternately, something they hoped for may not have the anticipated impact. For example, a patient may say that while psychotherapy has helped him remember and think about his life, it has been upsetting for him to come to realize the fragility of family members. In a similar vein, a patient may report that she can now think more clearly and is free of hallucinations but now feels overwhelmed by responsibilities she does not think she can meet.

With these types of reflections, patients can be seen forming and reforming ideas about themselves with the possibility of their leading to the formation of even more complex conceptualizations. As an illustration, the report of the patient who has fewer hallucinations and can now think more clearly is itself a metacognitive act. It is a reflection about what is happening in her mind and involves awareness of how this has changed relative to at least one point in the past. If the patient can link this change to, say, a growing sense of connection to the therapist and concurrent changes in her self-esteem, then we can see an even deeper metacognitive act. Here, not only is there awareness of changing mental states from past to present but an understanding of the interaction of those states with the world around her. Finally, a reflection that this change has had an unanticipated effect—for example, that it prompted an awareness of seemingly overwhelming responsibility—is still an even more complex metacognitive act. Not only is there awareness that her mental states are changing from past to present as a result of interaction with the world but also that these changes cause even more complicated changes in mental states.

Patient reflections about lack of progress require an open and welcoming response as should be the stance regardless of what the patient thinks about the session. Since negative patient perceptions may be interpreted by some therapists as an insult (either inadvertent or deliberate), criticism of their work, or evidence of professional inadequacy, these discussions can be particularly difficult for clinicians, especially if they are new to this work and still unsure of their abilities. Additionally, patients' critical responses about sessions may reflect an attempt to reject the stigmatizing role of the passive patient who should compliantly go along with what the therapist has in mind. Regardless of the underling dynamics, patients' perceptions should be respected and seen as personally meaningful acts and not necessarily personalized by clinicians.

In contrast, some patients may hesitate to share a criticism because of a fear of being seen as rude or unappreciative, or due to perceived differences in power within the relationship. As persons who have experienced extensive adversity and stigma, patients may not feel they have the right to offer critical thoughts about the session. Others may be overly eager to please and attempt to play of the role of the "good patient." Patients also may consider the therapist's time and attention as a gift and be reticent to critique any aspect of it for fear of appearing ungrateful. Alternately, patients may feel that if they criticize the therapist, the therapist may retaliate and criticize them. Thus, therapists should be prepared to offer only interest and encouragement in the face of genuine reflections about progress in sessions.

Regardless of whether progress is noted by the patient or not, therapists should ask about the factors which might explain this outcome. Therapists should accept they played a role in the lack of progress as well as not accept all the credit for positive change. As in all the other elements, the consideration about what has changed and not changed and why this is the case should be a matter of joint consideration. All change or lack of change should be generally considered as a reflection of the dyad with an emphasis on the patient's autonomy.

When no cause for lack of change can be found, it may be a signal for therapists to acknowledge that there is not an obvious answer at present but affirm that they will not give up and continue to meet with the patient. As a corollary, some patients may fear that the therapist will stop meeting with them if a great deal has been accomplished because their becoming well will cause treatment to end. Therapists should be aware of this possibility as well and be willing to offer reassurance that they do not plan to disengage because of observed gains.

Timing of Discussions About Progress

Inquiry about progress can occur at several different points and should not be scripted ahead of time. For instance, if the conversation has stalled and the patient's non-verbal behavior suggests distress, therapists can ask about how the session is going. Alternatively, patients' comments about how long they have been seeing the therapist could present an opportunity to reflect upon both specific and general progress.

Regardless of whether progress has been discussed early on or in the middle of a session, we do recommend asking patients for their appraisal of progress at the end of the session in a fashion that allows for sufficient time to discuss the patient's reaction. Additionally, when patients comment earlier in the session on progress, there may be good reason to query about this at the end of the session. We have observed that routinely asking for patients' appraisals of progress often leads their coming to do so spontaneously as a natural part of the session. Asking for a patient's perspective on progress in every session also communicates to patients that they have their own privileged view of things which can change and about which the therapist is not omniscient.

Synergy With the Other Elements

Element 5 calls for joint reflection on the therapeutic relationship because it is that context in which thinking about thinking takes place. This requires consideration of the position of the therapist within the therapeutic dialogue, reflections about how well the therapist is occupying that position, how helpful that position is, and how the patient reacts to the therapist in this role. Element 6 requires joint reflection about the effects of all five elements on the patient's mental states. These two elements, in contrast to the first four, call for larger scale reflections: reflection upon the interpersonal context in which reflection takes place (Element 5) and the effects of these lower level reflections (Element 6).

Together these two elements along with the first four continue to cast patients as agents who must form judgments about what is happening. It places their opinions on at least an equal footing with the therapist's and works against stigma or the formation of an unhealthy power differential. It also is another opportunity for joint consideration the about patients' reactions to what is happening in the moment.

This also illustrates how all of the MERIT elements are interrelated and cannot be expected to unfold or be pursued in a predetermined order because each can serve to amplify the other in a synergistic way. Successfully reflecting upon the relationship may open the door for consideration of progress where, for instance, consideration of whether the therapist's position is helpful may point to the question of what is or is not changing in the mind of the patient. Consideration of what is changing can raise the issue of the role of the therapeutic relationship. In turn, successfully thinking about the relationship and what is changing may lead to the discovery of new or obscured agendas, creating opportunities for therapists to insert their own mind, and reveal more narrative episodes and psychological problems.

MERIT-TAS Element 6

The MERIT Therapist Adherence Scale (MERIT-TAS) Element 6 scale can be found in Table 11.1. As noted in the table, satisfactory adherence to this element requires discussion of the progress within the session along with consideration of what has caused the progress. An optimal level of adherence requires discussion of the progress within session, its causes, and the effects of that progress (or its lack) on the patient (including patient reactions).

Table 11.1 MERIT-TAS Element 6 Scale

Score	*Level of Adherence*	*Therapist Behavior*
0	Absent	Failure to discuss progress or lack of progress within the session
1	Marginal	Discussion of the progress within the session
2	Satisfactory	Discussion of the progress within the session **with** consideration of what has caused the progress
3	Optimal	Discussion of the progress within session, its causes, **and** the effects of that progress or lack of progress on the patient (including patient reactions)

12 The MERIT-IF and Assessment of Metacognition During Sessions

MERIT Element 7 and Element 8 require that therapists use interventions that are offered at metacognitive levels which match but do not exceed patients' metacognitive capacities. These two elements are considered to be superordinate because they are concerned with therapeutic action across the whole of the session, regardless of the element or content. Element 7 focuses on patient perceptions of the self and others while Element 8 is concerned with whether and if so how patients are responding to psychosocial challenges with the use of metacognitive knowledge.

These two elements are at the core of MERIT's therapeutic action. They enable therapists to jointly reflect with patients about themselves and others and the use of that knowledge in a way that is metacognitively accessible to the patient. They allow therapists to appreciate the level of fragmentation of patients' experiences and understand the kinds of thoughts that can be shared productively. Ultimately, this continued joint reflection over time can to lead to the incremental growth in patients' metacognitive capacity.

In this chapter, we will focus on the methodology employed in MERIT for assessing the patient's capacity for metacognition within sessions. In the following chapter, we will review the types of interventions that are appropriate for each level of metacognition. We anticipate that most readers will have found the first six elements to be familiar. Likely each element can be found in some manner in most reader's current practice. The seventh and eight elements, however, may introduce new ways of conceptualizing those practices.

The MERIT Intervention Framework (MERIT-IF)

MERIT uses the MERIT Intervention Framework (MERIT-IF) to assess metacognition within sessions. As noted earlier, it was derived from the Metacognition Assessment Scale-Abbreviated (MAS-A). The MERIT-IF uses three scales to guide intervention: Self-Reflectivity (S), Understanding Others' Minds (O), and Mastery (M). It also includes the Decentration scale (D) for purposes of case conceptualization but not intervention. For each scale, the lowest level is labeled "0," and each successive higher level is conceptualized as involving a more complex integrative activity. The score on each scale is reflective of the patient's maximal capacity for metacognitive activity on that dimension. For example, a score of O4 indicates that the metacognitive activities detailed at that level are the most complex metacognitive activities a person can perform when thinking of specific other people.

The MERIT-IF Self-Reflectivity (S) Scale

The Self-Reflectivity (S) scale assesses the degree to which patients can form a relatively fragmented versus integrated and complex sense of themselves. The scale has ten levels, each of which involves a more complex integrative activity than the one before (see Table 12.1). Further, the ability to perform the metacognitive activity at a given level on the S scale requires the full ability to perform the metacognitive activity at the level beneath it. Consequently, a patient assessed as unable to perform the metacognitive ability at a given level cannot be assessed as performing the activity at the next level. For example, a patient assessed as unable to perform the metacognitive acts at S4 could not be assessed to be capable of performing the metacognitive acts described at S5.

The MERIT-IF Understanding Others' Minds (O) Scale

The Understanding Others' Minds (O) scale assesses the degree to which patients can form a relatively fragmented versus integrated and complex sense of other people. With consideration to other people, the MERIT-IF is referring to an awareness of a particular person or well-recognized group (e.g., family), not a nebulous, ill-defined reference to "they" or "other people," or persons the patient does not know in reality (e.g., a celebrity). This scale has eight levels; similar to the S scale, each level involves a more complex integrative activity than the one before (see Table 12.1). Further, the ability to perform the metacognitive activity at a given level on the O scale requires the full ability to perform the metacognitive activity at the level beneath it. Consequently, a patient assessed as unable to perform the metacognitive ability at a given level cannot be assessed as performing the activity at the next level. For example, a patient assessed as unable to perform the metacognitive acts at O4 could not be assessed to be capable of performing the metacognitive acts described at O5.

The MERIT-IF Mastery (M) Subscale

The Mastery (M) scale assesses the extent to which patients can use their metacognitive knowledge to respond to psychologically or emotionally challenging events. Each item on the Mastery scale reflects an increasingly complex use of metacognitive knowledge to respond to a real-life psychosocial challenge. This scale has ten intervals (see Table 12.3). For purposes of MERIT-IF scoring, *self-destructive attempts to reduce pain* are not understood as effective ways to cope and are not scored as examples of any level of Mastery. As can be seen

Table 12.1 Self-Reflectivity (S) Scale

S0: Unawareness of the experience of one's own mental activities Patients are unaware that they are having any thoughts or ideas. Patients who are catatonic or displaying extremely disorganized speech could receive this score.
S1: Awareness of mental activities but uncertainty whether they are one's own Patients are aware that they are having thoughts and ideas but not clearly understanding these as occurring within the boundary of the self. Patients who are experiencing pervasive thought insertion, thought broadcasting, or who cannot distinguish internal from external stimuli could receive this score.
S2: Awareness of mental experiences that are one's own Patients are aware that they are having thoughts and ideas which are occurring within the boundary of their own mind. Patients who can verbalize that they are having their own thoughts in the moment could receive this score.
S3: Recognition of distinct varied cognitive operations Patients are aware of their experience of different kinds of mental activities which are distinct from one another. Patients who can verbalize that they are having or making thoughts, plans, memories, hopes, desires, wishes, decisions, etc., could receive this score.
S4: Recognition of distinct varied emotional experiences Patients can name and distinguish their experience of different nuanced emotional states. Patients who can describe that they experience emotions such as anger, sadness, joy, happiness, surprise, despair, anxiety, shame, embarrassment, fear, frustration, guilt, hope, and jealousy could receive this score.
S5: Recognition that mental states are changing and that thoughts are subjective and fallible Patients are aware that what they think may later prove to be untrue or that they may hold different beliefs at different times. Patients who acknowledge that they believe a certain thing but realize they could change their mind or feel differently over time could receive this score.
S6: Recognition that hopes and wishes are potentially not aligned with reality Patients can distinguish fantasy from reality and accept instances where they are at odds. Patients who are aware that the confines of reality may not allow those hopes and dreams to be actualized could receive this score.
S7: Recognition of the mutual influence of one's thoughts, wishes, feelings, and/or behavior upon one another within a narrative episode Patients can talk about how different mental states are influencing each other within a specific situation. Patients who can talk about how emotions and thoughts affect each other in the midst of a specific time could receive this score.
S8: Recognition of the mutual influence of one's thoughts, wishes, feelings, and/or behavior upon one another across and between narrative episodes Patients can recognize patterns of functioning over time and stitch together different episodes to form a personal narrative which spans at least two events. Patients who can talk about how different emotions and thoughts affect each other in similar ways across different distinct moments in their lives could receive this score.
S9: Integration of multiple narratives to create a coherent and complex personal narrative Patients are able to integrate multiple aspects of self-experience (e.g., emotional, cognitive, behavioral, interpersonal, and developmental), allowing them to see themselves as a multifaceted being across the course of their lives. Patients who can talk about their lives in terms of their life story and make sense of their personal history in a multifaceted manner could receive this score.

Table 12.2 Understanding Others' Minds (O) Scale

O0: Unawareness of others' experience of mental activities
Patients are unaware that others are having any thoughts or ideas. Patients who are withdrawn to the point of autism, or those who appear to have no representations of others as having their own subjective experience could receive this score.

O1: Awareness of others' mental activities but uncertainty whether they are their own
Patients are aware that others are having thoughts and ideas but do not clearly understand that these thoughts are occurring within the boundary of the self. Patients who believe others are subject to pervasive thought insertion, or thought broadcasting, could receive this score.

O2: Awareness of others' mental experiences that are their own
Patients are aware that others are having thoughts and ideas which are occurring within the boundary of their own mind. Patients who can verbalize that others are having their own thoughts in the moment could receive this score.

O3: Recognition that others experience distinct varied cognitive operations
Patients are aware that others experience different kinds of mental activities which are distinct from one another. Patients who can verbalize that others are having or making thoughts, plans, memories, hopes, desires, wishes, decisions, etc., could receive this score.

O4: Recognition that others have distinct varied emotional experiences
Patients can name and distinguish others' experience of different nuanced emotional states. Patients who can describe that others experience emotions such as anger, sadness, joy, happiness, surprise, despair, anxiety, shame, embarrassment, fear, frustration, guilt, hope, and jealousy could receive this score.

O5: Recognition of others' changing mental states used to make inferences about the intentions of other people
Patients are able to make hypotheses about the cognitive and emotional functioning of others based on verbal or non-verbal cues. Patient who can guess what others want of them and those around them could receive this score.

O6: Recognition of the mutual influence of another's thoughts, wishes, feelings, and/or behavior upon one another within a narrative episode
Patients can talk about how different mental states of an other are influencing each other within a specific situation. Patients who can talk about how the emotions and thoughts of an other affect each other in the midst of a specific time could receive this score.

O7: Recognition of the mutual influence of thoughts, wishes, feelings, and/or behavior upon one another across narrative episodes
Patients can construct a fluid narrative with obvious integration of multiple emotional, cognitive, behavioral, interpersonal, and developmental factors. Patients who can integrate multiple aspects of the other person (e.g., emotional, cognitive, behavioral, interpersonal, and developmental), which allows them to see the other person as a multifaceted being across the course of his or her life, could receive this score.

Table 12.3 Mastery (M) Scale

M0: No identified distress or psychological problems
Patients cannot express any kind of emotional distress or challenge they are facing.

M1: Implausible psychological or social problems
Patients can name some form of challenge they face but attribute it to a cause or describe it in a manner that is unusual, fantastic, or incoherent to the extent that others in the patient's community would not accept. Although they do not describe a clear and plausible psychological challenge, they will describe some sort of distress.

M2: Plausible psychological or social problems
Patients can name some form of challenge they face and not attribute it to a cause or describe it in a manner that is unusual, fantastic, or incoherent to the extent that others in the patient's community would not accept.

M3: Reduce distress through use of passive and grossly avoidant strategies
Patients can respond to distress resulting from psychological or social challenges through either completely withdrawing or passively following directions from another person.

M4: Reduce distress through selective avoidance or interpersonal support
Patients can decide to avoid one specific thing or turn to an other for comfort, while continuing to stay generally engaged in life.

M5: Active response to distress through behavioral strategies
Patients refer to engaging in specific behaviors to manage psychological and social challenges. This can include, for example, deciding to exercise, practice relaxation techniques, eat healthier meals, etc. Of note, passively choosing behaviors at the direction of others is a reflection of an earlier level (M3) and should be scored as such.

M6: Active response to distress through altering thoughts
Patients are able to respond to psychological and social problems by altering how they think about them. This can include, for example, using adaptive self-statements to replace maladaptive ones or reframe a problematic situation in a more positive or realistic way.

M7: Active response to distress through use of unique metacognitive knowledge of oneself
Patients can respond to psychosocial challenges using an understanding of how their beliefs, perceptions, expectations, and thoughts interact and how those processes have contributed to the development and maintenance of the psychosocial challenge.

M8: Active response to distress through use of unique metacognitive knowledge of oneself and others
Patients can respond to psychosocial challenges using an understanding of the interaction of theirs and others' beliefs, perceptions, expectations, and thoughts and how those processes have contributed to the development and maintenance of the psychosocial challenge.

M9: Active response to distress through use of unique metacognitive knowledge of oneself, others, and the human condition
Patients use their metacognitive awareness of themselves and others as well as acceptance that distress and conflict are part of the human condition and cannot be entirely avoided.

in the criteria, ratings of 2 or higher require that the patient has a plausible psychological problem, so patients without a plausible psychological problem can only be given a rating or 1 or 0.

The MERIT-IF Decentration (D) Subscale

The Decentration (D) scale assesses the extent to which a patient can recognize that other people lead lives which may intersect his but are independent of the patient who is not necessarily the center of others' lives (see Table 12.4). It reflects the ability of patients to situate their ideas of themselves in the larger social world. As in the case of S and O, each level involves a more complex integrative activity than the one before. Further, the ability to perform the metacognitive activity at a given level on the D scale requires the full ability to perform the metacognitive activity at the level beneath it. For example, patients assessed as not capable of D1 cannot be assessed as capable of D2.

Assessing Metacognition in Psychotherapy Sessions With the MERIT-IF

Elements 7 and 8 require therapists make continuous assessments of S, O, and M, as well as D, throughout the session. Ongoing assessment is necessary because metacognitive capacity may change during a session. For example, a person may initially be able to distinguish mental contents but not emotions (S3) in a narrative but become able to notice and distinguish different emotions (S4) as a session progresses. Alternatively, patients may experience a decline in functioning if psychic pain emerges in discussing a memory, for

Table 12.4 Decentration (D) Scale

D0: All activities are related to the self.
Patients cannot recognize that they are not the center of all meaningful or noteworthy activity. Patients are unable to describe events as being unrelated to them.

D1: There are activities unrelated to the self.
Patients can recognize that events can occur without reference to themselves and that others may say or do things which are not related to the patient.

D2: Events can be seen from multiple valid perspectives.
Patients can see that others have valid ways of understanding an event that may differ from their own.

D3: Life events are often the result of complex factors that vary from person to person.
Patients are able to sustain a sense of themselves and others as existing in a larger world where individuals have unique relationships with one another that do not have a central organizing theme. Patients can see others having unique relationships with each other that do not involve the patient.

example moving from being able to notice others' emotions to a having a limited awareness of others' mental states (O4 to O2).

Assessment should be carried out organically within the natural flow of the conversation during sessions when addressing any of MERIT's first six elements. For example, the patient's capacity for metacognition can and should be assessed when talking about the agenda, the patient's reaction to the therapist, a narrative episode, the psychological problem, and the experience of change. Metacognition can also be assessed when the patient is merely talking about himself or others.

Therapists should generally not seek to assess metacognition by asking direct questions about it. For example, in trying to decide if a patient has a nuanced sense of his or her emotions, therapists should avoid asking, "Do you have a nuanced sense of your emotions?" Similarly, if the therapist seeks to understand if the patient knows his thoughts are subjective, the initial approach to assessing this should not be to ask, "Do you know your thoughts are subjective?" Instead, therapists should look for evidence of these capacities within the flow of conversation (e.g., in the use of affect-laden words or descriptions of states which indicate the patient doubts her thoughts). While there may be times when it is useful to note, "It seems like you cannot name your emotions right now," or "It is hard to imagine there is another way to see things," the onus is on the therapist to assess the metacognitive capacities that are evident in what is transpiring in the moment in sessions, not by asking for the patient's direct report.

The assessment of metacognition should be a matter of intuition but also closely informed by consideration of the patient's verbal and non-verbal communication, the therapists' own memories of previous sessions, as well as reactions to the patient. The therapist's judgment is crucial because she is called upon to go beyond the face value of what a patient has said and try to *understand what the patient means and intends when he says a particular thing.* This requires the clinician to form a complex integrated idea about the patient and then judge what level of metacognitive activity that patient is capable of in the moment. Stated in another way, the clinician has to be continuously making complex metacognitive judgments about patients' capacities. It is also expected that clinicians will make errors in their assessments and that they can and should be revised if need be as the session unfolds. For instance, a patient may appear able to describe a narrative episode in detail and be seen as functioning at S7, but if it becomes apparent that he is only using rationalization and lacks a nuanced awareness of emotional experience, a more accurate appraisal would be S3.

As a general rule, clinicians must also make judgments about the *authenticity* of a patient's statements. They must judge if a patient is pretending, feigning, or just saying what he or she thinks is expected. To this point, there are times when we all respond to questions based on what we believe others want to hear. Furthermore, years of repetitive psychiatric treatment can have the effect of "teaching" or indoctrinating patients to respond in certain ways. For example, it is not an uncommon clinical experience to ask a patient diagnosed with schizophrenia if she thinks she has a mental illness and hear, "I have schizophrenia." However, when asked what that means, the patient may say, "I don't know, it's what my doctor tells me." That being said, these assessment procedures do not ask clinicians to be suspicious, distrustful, or to act like detectives. However, what we do wish to impress upon the reader is that the use of the MERIT-IF requires complex thought on the part of the clinician. These are not methods where simple questions are asked and the responses recorded.

Assessing Self-Reflectivity With the S Scale

To assess S, therapists should *focus on patients' verbalizations in which they are talking about themselves.* A common beginning point is to look for verbalizations which suggest patients are capable of self-reflection (S3), an awareness that they not only have their own thoughts but can also distinguish the different kinds of mental activities or cognitive operations they are experiencing. Patient verbalizations such as: "I remembered/wished/wanted/planned" are evidence that patients are able to see that there are different kinds of mental activities occurring in their minds. Additionally, the content of the verbalization has to be plausible. As a result, reporting a psychic ability should not be assessed as having awareness of a cognitive operation.

If patients seem incapable of metacognitive activity at S3, it would be assumed they are not capable of metacognitive activity at the next level, S4. As a result, therapists should look for verbalizations that suggest the patient is capable of self-reflectivity activity at S2 which would be verbalizations suggesting that the patient is aware that she has mental activities which are her own. Evidence that patients are aware that there are mental activities occurring in their own mind would include gross and undifferentiated statements indicating something is occurring within boundaries of their consciousness (e.g., "I am all just confusion" or "My thoughts are running all together").

Though rather uncommon, some patients may not show evidence of S2, in which case therapists should assess for S1, which reflects an awareness of mental activities but without a clear boundary defining whether their mental activities are internal or external events. Examples of verbalizations at this level would include statements that locate the patient's own thoughts as occurring externally (e.g., being broadcast from a television or actions being controlled by a machine or supernatural source). Patients who do not show evidence of S1 would be unaware that they have any mental events at all, as might be found in patients with catatonia or who are severely withdrawn or profoundly disorganized. This would result in a rating of S0.

However, if patients do achieve S3, therapists should assess whether S4 is present which is being able to notice their own experience of nuanced emotions. Verbalizations which suggest this include the naming of a range of different emotions (e.g. "I felt sad/pleased/scared/jealous, etc."). Patients capable of naming only one emotion or emotions which are closely related (e.g., "I felt angry/enraged/irritated, etc.") would not be seen as capable of performing at S4 and higher levels of S should not be considered.

If a patient is capable of S4, then the presence of S5 should be assessed. Evidence of this includes verbalizations suggesting awareness of the flow of consciousness and the subjectivity and fallibility of thought. Example of these verbalizations would include: "I used to think x but now I see I was wrong" and "I feel certain about x but I realize I could be wrong." Patients who can only realize that others think that the patient is fallible but do not doubt their own thinking themselves would not be assessed as meeting this level. Additionally, a concrete example of a person's specific thoughts being fallible is required, not just an abstract statement about the possibility of fallibility (e.g., "I know I'm not perfect") for this level to be met.

Patients assessed as capable of S5 should be assessed for S6, which reflects an awareness that one's own mental states and needs do not always match what is possible given the dictates of reality. At this level, patients are aware of their emotional states and can contrast that with what is possible in the world or reality. Examples of verbalizations which suggest patients are capable of this include "I hoped for that but I know it is not possible" and "I wish that person x felt a certain way but I don't think she does."

If the criteria for S6 are met, the therapist should consider S7, which reflects the ability to integrate thoughts, affects, changing mental states, and the requirements of reality as they occur within a specific narrative episode. This requires the patient to describe an interaction of mental states within her mind as they are occurring and include a well-defined set of details that are linked together within a single event. An example of this is a patient's description of how her emotions led her to jump to a conclusion about a family picnic or exchange with a work supervisor last week.

If S7 is assessed as met, the therapist should consider S8, which reflects the ability to not only talk about the interaction of mental activities within a narrative episode but to link that episode to other narratives. An example which supports this would include a patient's description of how her thoughts and feelings influenced one another at a family picnic and also how it is similar to what happened in another well-defined narrative episode (e.g., how her thoughts and feelings influenced each other in a recently ended romantic relationship).

If patients are capable of S8, then S9 should be assessed, which is the ability to connect multiple narrative episodes and/or thematically organized groups of narratives into a larger life story. Verbalizations which indicate this would be complex personal narratives which have temporal continuity and span large portions of a person's life.

Assessing Awareness of the Other With the O Scale

To assess O, therapists should focus on *verbalizations in which patients are talking about specific other people (e.g., a sister, named friend, supervisor, neighbor, etc.)*. Verbalizations that refer to "they" or to "people," or in other words, a non-specific person or particular group, would not be considered as evidence of capacity for O. As in the assessment of S, a common beginning point is to look for verbalizations which suggest patients are aware that others not only have their own thoughts but can also distinguish the different kinds of mental activities or cognitive operations that other people experience (O3). Patient verbalizations such as "He remembered/wished/wanted/planned" are evidence that patients are able to see that different kinds of mental activities are occurring in another person's mind. If patients seem incapable of O3, it would be assumed they are not capable of O4. As is the case of S, the content of a patient's verbalization must be *plausible* for it to be seen as evidence of a metacognitive capacity (e.g., believing others have psychic abilities would not be taken as evidence of awareness of others' cognitive operations).

If patients are incapable of O3, then therapists should look for patients' verbalizations that suggest they are capable of O2 level metacognition, which is an awareness that others have mental activities of their own. This could include broad statements indicating something is occurring within boundaries of the consciousness of the other (e.g., "He has thoughts" or "She decided to watch me").

Though somewhat unusual, some patients may not achieve O2. In this situation, therapists should assess for the O1, which is an awareness that others have mental activities but without a clear awareness whether these are internal or external events. Examples of this would include statements that locate other people's thinking as occurring externally, such as that thoughts are being broadcast from a television or actions are being caused by an external source. Patients unable to function at this level would be those who are unaware that others have any mental events at all, as might be found in patients with catatonia or who are severely delusional, withdrawn, or profoundly disorganized. They would be seen as functioning at O0.

If patients are able to achieve O3, therapists should assess whether they are capable of O4, having the capacity to notice that others experience nuanced emotions. Verbalizations which suggest this include the naming of a range of different emotions (e.g., "She felt sad/pleased/scared/jealous"). Patients who are only capable of naming one emotion or emotions which are closely related (e.g., "She felt angry/enraged/irritated") would not be seen as demonstrating function at O3 level and higher levels of O would not be considered.

If a patient is capable of O4, then O5 should be assessed, which is the ability to see that others' mental states may change and the patient can make judgments about what others want and need on the basis their non-verbal and verbal behavior. Here, there is not just an understanding of the other but also that the other is communicating something to the patient. Evidence that a patient has attained O5 includes verbalizations such as: "The reason she said x was that she really wanted me to do y" or "From the way he was acting, I realize that he was trying to get me to understand z."

Patients able to carry out metacognitive acts at the O5 level should be assessed for whether they are capable of metacognitive act at the O6 level, the ability to piece together others' thoughts, affects, and changing mental states as they are occurring within a specific narrative episode. Evidence that the patient is capable of this requires the patient to describe the interaction of mental states within the mind of another specific person as they are occurring within a well-defined set of events that are linked together within a single time frame. An example of this would be a patient describing how her friend's emotions led him to jump to a conclusion in an interaction with a family member at a social event.

If the O6 is present, the therapist should assess whether the patient is capable of O7, which is not only the ability to talk about the interaction of another person's mental activities within a narrative episode but also to link that episode to other narratives of that person's life. An example of this would be the patient who not only described how another person's thoughts and feelings influenced one another at a family social event but also how this same pattern of interaction of thoughts and feelings is similar to what happened to her friend in another well-defined narrative episode (e.g., in a conflict with his girlfriend last month).

Assessing Mastery With the M Scale

Assessing the M scale begins by looking for evidence about *whether the patient recognizes that she has a psychological or social problem and whether that problem is plausible.* Examples of psychological or social problems with a plausible cause include feeling lonely, frightened, bereft of social status, longing for companionship, or fearing rejection. Examples of problems without a plausible cause are feelings of uncertainty and fear attributed to witches or lack of social status due the persecution by the Mafia.

Of note, *patients do not need to be free of delusions to have a plausible problem.* For instance, a patient might hear voices and attribute that to supernatural forces but also realistically represent how isolated he feels due to having low social rank or little sense of importance or standing in his community. Similarly, it is also possible for patients who have little to no awareness that they are mentally ill to be able to identify a problem with a plausible cause. For instance, the patient says she is not ill in any way but has felt alone and desperate since she started hearing voices would be said to have a psychological problem which has a plausible cause.

If an individual can identify no psychological or social problems whatsoever, she would be assessed as functioning at M0. These are patients who are not aware of anything plausible or implausible that has gone wrong in their lives or brought them distress. Here, we are not referring to a lack of reflectivity in general. Rather, M0 pertains only to those instances in which there is denial of *both* mental illness and the denial of the experience of any form of distress or psychological challenge (e.g., patient who has not worked in decades, has no social connections, has been hospitalized several times, and has experienced homelessness for extended periods but definitively states she is not experiencing any problems). The patient who does identify a psychological or social problem but offers an implausible explanation for it would be seen as functioning at M1.

However, if a patient is able to identify a psychological or social problem that has a plausible cause, the clinician should next assess the capacity for using metacognitive knowledge to respond to these problems and assign the score that best describes these abilities. A score of M2 is appropriate if a patient has no response of any sort to the psychological or social challenge he is facing. Verbalizations that suggest M2 include those which describe the problem as something inevitable and unavoidable. This might be exemplified by the patient who believes he was fated to feel hated and belittled by others and believes that he has no way to respond to it whatsoever. Patients assessed at M2 typically appear to be frozen or helpless in the face of distress.

M3 is assigned when patients respond to psychological or social problems by means of passive and grossly avoidant measures. An example is the patient who responds to feeling socially marginalized or plagued with odd experiences by rarely leaving his apartment. In contrast to a patient assessed as M2, someone with the capacity for M3 might report: "It was overwhelming, so I sat in the dark in my apartment for the rest of the day."

Evidence that patients are capable of M4 includes verbalizations describing how they have responded to a psychological problem either by seeking support from others or by doing something to actively avoid a very specific aspect of the problem. Examples of verbalizations which support this include: "I was overwhelmed, so I went to spend time with my aunt" or "I decided to avoid the state fair to avoid feelings that I might be being judged." For a patient to be capable of M5, there should be verbalizations which indicate she has used a specific behavior strategy to respond to a psychological and social challenge she faces. Examples of this include patients who say they have decided to exercise regularly or who have taken certain behavioral steps to get needed levels of sleep so as to not be overwhelmed by their problems.

The MERIT-IF also distinguishes persons who actively pursue psychiatric treatment and take a meaningful role in managing their own care from those who passively follow orders. Patients who take an active role in determining with their provider what the best combination of medications is for them and then carefully adhering to those medicines as a way to reduce symptoms or keep them at bay are seen as capable of M5. However, patients who report they merely do as they are told are assessed as capable of M3.

Evidence of capacity at M6 includes verbalizations about how the patient responds to a psychological or social problem by adjusting how he is thinking. Examples of this include the person who decides to prepare for a difficult conversation by thinking about it in a less pessimistic way or the patient with paranoia who has just come to realize that she can no longer be certain that her suspicions about the neighbor's son are true.

While M6 refers to the capacity to modify specific beliefs, evidence that patients are capable of M7 includes describing the ability to respond to problems based on their unique knowledge of themselves. The patient who says, "I need to stop ruminating about that insult" would be assessed as capable of Mastery at the M6 level. In contrast, the person at M7 might say, "I have to stop ruminating about that insult because I'm overly sensitive to rejection and tend to exaggerate possible slights." Similarly, patients are capable of M8 if they are able to utilize both the larger understanding of themselves found in M7 and a unique understanding of the others involved. An example of this would be the patient who not only tries to avoid ruminating because he realizes that he overreacts but also tries to understand the mental state of the person whom he feels may have slighted him. Finally, M9 should be offered if there is evidence in the patient's verbalizations of the use of unique knowledge of self and others and of the larger community when responding to psychological and social challenges. Evidence of M9 might include a person who recognizes the effects of childhood sexual trauma on herself and her past relationships with others and accepts the limitations that come with this history without foreclosing on the ability to find meaning and fulfillment in life.

Assessing Decentration With the D Scale

While Decentration is not used to plan interventions, it is assessed for case conceptualization purposes. Patients are assessed as functioning at D0 if they cannot imagine that all the events around them are not related to them. Examples of patients who function at D0 include those who feel everyone in a restaurant is looking at them or that the words in a sermon at church were chosen specially and exclusively for them. Importantly, assessing a patient at D0 indicates that he is not seen as capable of realizing that others have motives and internal states that are unrelated to him.

Evidence someone is capable of D1 would include even very simple verbalizations that suggest motives unrelated to the patient. For example, a patient capable of D1 might note: "My mother is sad since it is the anniversary of my grandmother's death" or "The waiter at the restaurant had a funny expression on his face. I wonder if he was feeling okay."

Assessment of D2 should be made when the person not only realizes that others act in ways unrelated to him but have valid views which differ from his own. An example would be: "My sister sees our family in a different way than I do and notices things I sometimes miss." Patients who merely state that others see things differently but also clearly dismiss those alternative views as incorrect would not be seen as functioning at D2. Finally, a level of D3 is present when patients verbalize an awareness that others not only have their own motives and unique and valid worldviews but also have complex relationships with others that are completely independent of the patient.

Considerations When Using the MERIT-IF

In outlining how to use the MERIT-IF, we have described a step-by-step process in which each level of a scale is considered sequentially for clarity of presentation. In reality, though, there can be quite a bit of variability in the time and attention that is needed to carry out the process. There will be situations in which it is readily apparent from the patient's first series of sentences that she is capable of higher levels of S, O, and M. For example, she may quickly share a narrative that describes her thoughts and feelings as interacting, makes reasonable inferences about others on the basis of their non-verbal behavior, and contemplates how she needs to address an issue she is facing, making it readily apparent that she is capable of S7, O5, and M6. Other times, it may take considerable effort and thought for the therapist to form a clear idea about the patient's metacognitive capacity.

While we have discussed assessing patients' metacognitive capacities largely based upon their spontaneous verbalizations, much can also be gleaned from how patients respond to questions and reflections. For example, a patient may use many words that describe emotions and appear to be capable of S4. However, when asked about what he feels, he may present with confusion and uncertainty and lead the therapist to consider revising the initial assessment. Therapists should also be mindful that since metacognitive capacity can change over the course of a session, it is important to attend to the assessment process whenever they are with a patient.

13 Element 7

Stimulating Self-Reflection (S) and Awareness of the Other (O)

Like the development of any ability, the capacity to engage in metacognition will increase with practice. One of MERIT's key principles is that stimulating patients to think about themselves and others at their maximal metacognitive capacity within a safe, predictable, non-judgmental, yet provocative, space will optimally foster the development of that capacity. Element 7 requires that S and O be stimulated at a level consistent with the patients' metacognitive capacity while Element 8 specifies that M also be stimulated at the maximally optimal level.

Clinicians should use the MERIT-IF throughout each session to determine the patient's capacities for S and O. This is critical information because interventions that ask patients to think at levels beyond which they are capable are unlikely to be helpful and may even be detrimental. For example, if patients have not yet developed (or recaptured) the capacity to think about the experience of nuanced emotion (S4), asking them to think about different feelings would likely be ineffective and feel foreign, too abstract, or impersonal. Similarly, if patients cannot recognize the feelings of others (O4), asking them to do something they are incapable of or cannot comprehend will almost inevitably prove a frustrating task.

MERIT focuses on using interventions that spur patients to think at the most complex level they are capable in order to "exercise" and continue to develop their metacognitive abilities. This process encourages patients to use their metacognitive capacities much in the way a physical therapist works with individuals who have an orthopedic injury by asking them to gradually engage in more challenging tasks as they become stronger and their condition improves. In both cases, using interventions that exceed the patient's current abilities are to be avoided because of the risk of injury and clinical setback. In order to facilitate clinical growth, the clinician must closely attend to the patient's condition in the moment and encourage those activities that are most likely to be effective.

The following section will review the types of interventions that are appropriate for each level of S and O as well as how progress on these dimensions of the MERIT-IF might be manifested. Therapists should be aware that while Element 7 considers both S and O, the relative emphasis on S and O will vary

Table 13.1 Characteristic Outcomes and Interventions for Self-Reflection (S)

Level	*Outcome*	*Interventions*
S1	Realizing one has mental experiences	• *There is a thought that . . .* • *You are seeing . . .*
S2	Realizing one's mental experiences are one's own	• *There is tension in your body . . .* • *There is an idea in your head that . . .*
S3	Noticing one's own recent and distal memories and immediate experiences as something the person has uniquely and subjectively experienced	• *You are recalling . . .* • *You had a plan to. . . .* • *You chose not to . . .* • *You are imagining . . .*
S4	Imbuing of one's own life events and/or experiences in the moment with different emotions	• *Now you are feeling . . .* • *Your feelings have changed.* • *You have two different feelings about . . .*
S5	Understanding one's own thoughts, emotions, and wishes as changing and shifting within the flow of life	• *You have changed your mind about . . .* • *You were certain before but not now about . . .*
S6	Understanding life events as involving realities that interact with one's own needs that emerge from changing mental states	• *You wish so much for . . . but it is not so.* • *You have discovered things are different than you needed.*
S7, S8, S9	Complete and rich descriptions of oneself in single events, across different events, and across the span of one's life respectively	• *Your thoughts and feelings were connected when . . .* • *Your thoughts were connected to your feelings both times . . .* • *Across your life your thoughts and feelings have . . .*

not only between patients but also at different times in treatment for the same patient. Table 13.1 summarizes the interventions and typical outcomes per each level of the S scale.

Stimulating S

Patients Not Capable of S1

Patients who are not capable of S1 are among the most impaired. They may be in a near catatonic state or speak in such a cacophonous or disorganized manner that they are unable to produce a narrative episode or frame a psychological problem. Regardless, consistent with what Prouty (2003) has called pre-therapy, appropriate intervention is still likely to be valuable. This might include noticing that an otherwise catatonic patient has moved her hand or looked at her watch. Similarly, the therapist might observe that an individual speaking in a non-stop manner paused briefly when he had to take a breath or that the patient seems to want the therapist to be silent. As noted by Searles (1965) and many others, it can be extremely uncomfortable to sit with someone who is in such a state. However, the ability for a clinician to master her anxiety during such moments may be a precondition for success in forming the roots of a relationship. Additionally, treating patients courteously and seeing them as dignified human beings capable of making sense of the world is also needed to start the process of developing a shared dialogue.

Patients Capable of S1 and S2

Patients at S1 and S2 are persons who are uncertain if they have thoughts in their head or if the thoughts they experience are their own, respectively. These patients require the most basic interventions that will serve to locate mental events in their minds. The only difference between the two levels is that at S2, mental events are understood as explicitly being those of the patient whereas the patient at S1 is struggling to see that things are occurring in his mind.

Interventions appropriate for patients at S1 consist of reflections that they are having specific thoughts while those for patients at S2 should recognize that those thoughts do belong to them. For instance, for a patient at S1 who has just described a plethora of persecutory thoughts, an appropriate intervention might be: "Your mind is full of thoughts about people persecuting you." For the patient at S2, it might be: "In your mind, you hear the voices and now we are talking about them." By contrast, for a patient at S1 who has few thoughts, the therapist might listen for instances in which the patient has formed a thought and merely highlight this by saying, "Today, there are thoughts about x in your mind." For patients at S2, the therapist might respond to instances in which the patient has formed a thought that she seems to recognize is uniquely her own: "Right now you are thinking x." All of these interventions invite patients to form ideas about themselves that might be shared with the therapist and assist them to make the very essential distinctions which allow their minds to be a subject of reflection.

For patients at S2, an element of mild confrontation may emerge when reflecting about how they are thinking about their own mental experiences. For instance, listening and noticing how a patient is characterizing his thoughts, a therapist might note: "You seem so certain about x, like there is nothing more to be said about that" or "You seem to have two different ideas about this." These interventions are not intended to highlight potentially dysfunctional beliefs (which would require a greater capacity for self-reflectivity) but rather provide an opportunity for patients to notice something about a belief that is their own.

When focusing on the therapy relationship, intervention for patients at this level can focus on observations about the patient. For example, a therapist might notice for a patient at S1: "You smiled when you first saw me," or at S2: "It is not comfortable for you to be here today." Appropriate reflections about therapeutic progress for S1 include: "There were different thoughts in your head today," while an appropriate reflection about progress at S2 might be: "For you, things are not working here today." As can be seen in these examples, patients are asked to form an idea of themselves at a level of complexity that they can understand.

Evidence of progress for patients at S1 often begins with verbalization of an awareness that they are forming ideas and thinking in the midst of specific experiences. It should be noted that the elementary fragments of experience introduced by patients at this level might be later woven into the threads necessary for the emergence of personal narrative at S2. Evidence of progress to S2 includes patients verbalizing that they see themselves, albeit in small fragments, as agents who are passive observers and responders to their experiences. This growing personal awareness can lead to pain because it may highlight a sense of profound emptiness. In such cases, the intervention might be something like: "You have no thoughts now," which affords patients the opportunity to recognize that they can detect the absence of thoughts in their minds.

Patients Capable of S3

At S3, patients are capable of recognizing that they use different cognitive operations. Conversations at this level will be significant for the nuanced naming of different emotions and cognitive operations. Interventions can include listening for when the patient is reporting a memory or planning something and then saying: "You are having a memory" or "You are forming a plan to . . ."

As an illustration, a patient functioning at S3 spontaneously mentioned a historical detail in the midst of a narrative episode. In response, the therapist offered: "You are remembering something about yourself ten years ago." This assisted the patient to recognize the presence of a specific cognitive operation and led to a richer narrative episode in which he recalled being bullied in high school. With reflection about how the patient was having memories, he started to be able to distinguish the act of having a memory from other cognitive operations such as making plans for his future.

Interventions can also focus on the emerging therapeutic relationship—for instance: "So this is something you planned yesterday to make sure and tell me" and "X was something you remembered from our last conversation." Patients may also bring up something from a past session with or without clearly remembering the actual conversation. Interventions which use the second person "you" and point to specific cognitive operations may serve to help patients to recognize different aspects of their thought processes. With practice, patients become more able to perform these kinds of metacognitive acts in their daily interactions.

Evidence of progress at S3 includes patient verbalizations about isolated episodes of their life. While progress at S1 and S2 is reflected in the emergence of fragments, parts of a story that are uniquely the patient's own may become available at S3. Metaphorically, the atoms of experience that emerged in the first two stages become the molecules that are assembled into a coherent but brief narrative. This experience may cause distress as patients rely less on delusions to explain their experiences and come to experience themselves in a more realistic manner.

Patients Capable of S4

Interventions for patients assessed at S4 should be geared toward encouraging them to recognize and distinguish different emotions. Here, the therapist can listen for the patient to share aspects of an emotional experience that represents a genuine emotional experience and not just the use of words that describe emotions. Here, a reflection might be offered such as: "You're feeling x" or "You are having a strong emotion right now." The goal of this intervention is not for the patient to attain knowledge of a specific state but to develop the capacity to be aware that emotions are part of her subjective experience. Additionally, it would be a positive sign if the patient responded to this intervention with, "No, you are wrong. It's more like I feel x and y." S4 may also be stimulated with confrontation when emotions seem to be absent but the patient appears capable of experienced nuanced emotion. Here, to stimulate the patient to reflect upon her emotions the therapist might note: "You are talking endlessly about your feeling persecuted so you don't have to feel sad" or "As you've grown quiet for a moment you are feeling something strongly." Finally, in the beginning stages of this process, the emotion may be experienced but difficult to clearly label, for example, "I feel like I did when my brother died." For those who are functioning at S3, but having more of a difficult time with S4, it can be helpful to focus on affective states that are associated with memories which may function as a "stepping stone" to naming emotions in the moment.

Interventions which stimulate S4 can also be tied to the therapeutic relationship. For example, while disclosing emotions to the therapist, the patient may also experience a mix of emotions about the therapist including admiration, attachment, and jealousy. Discussing this material can serve the purpose of not only strengthening the relationship but spurring the awareness of nuanced emotion.

Evidence of progress at this level includes the development of increasingly detailed accounts of both positive and negative emotions. There may be

Patients Capable of S7, S8, and S9

At S7, S8, and S9, patients are able to see themselves as having a variety of different cognitive operations and nuanced interacting emotions as well as an understanding of the difference in single moments (S7), across moments (S8), and through their lives holistically (S9). Here, therapist interventions should cue patients to form complex ideas of themselves within single narrative episodes or across narrative episodes. At this level of S, therapists often need to be less active than at lower levels of S. The goal remains to think with patients about how they are thinking about themselves. However, rather than focusing on specific elements such as whether there is a memory, how two feelings differ, or uncertainty about a specific thing, the narratives should be sufficiently broad with the patient situated as the protagonist.

When intervening at this level, therapists should actively consider themes that might link narrative episodes and result in interventions that may be more interpretive than reflective. This may include therapists offering thoughts about larger patterns within and across narratives and then allowing patients to respond to and expand those potential larger structures. Linking the themes across discrete narrative episodes assists patients in moving from S7 to S8, just as linking a theme over an even longer time span will help patients move from S8 to S9. As an illustration, a patient spoke about how her fears of rejection and being forever alone interfered with a conversation she had with a new lover (S7). When asked about how this related to other events in her life, she was able to identify other times when comfort with the sick role had similarly interfered in her life when she introduced herself as a schizophrenic and potential romantic partners quickly lost interest in her. The therapist helped the patient to think about how she had thought of herself as someone who always felt inferior to others, anticipated failure, and saw withdrawal and subtle forms of self-sabotage as the safest lifelong option (S9).

Exploring the dynamics of interpersonal relatedness continues to be critical at S9. At lower levels of S there may have been fears of simply being known by the therapist. By contrast, at S9 the patient may need to explore their experiences with the therapist as a specific person who knows them and who holds them accountable. In parallel fashion, as patients' representations of themselves grow more complex, there will be greater opportunities for the patient to be known in a complex manner by others.

Evidence of progress in these higher levels of S includes the production of narratives in which patients have complex and dynamic internal experiences which follow observable patterns over time where events are linked to patient intentions and not just caused by other events. At S9, a dynamic of self-compassion may emerge in which there is a non-judgmental account and understanding of one's own limitations over the course of life.

Common Challenges in Making S Interventions

One common challenge therapists experience is the emergence of events or acute problems that distract from the in-session assessment of S. For example, therapists may feel compelled to "fix" something for the patient and lose focus on whether their interventions are at the appropriate level. It is also not unusual for patients to directly ask for help with something. When patients say things like, "I am here for you to solve my depression" or "When will you start to tell me what to do?" therapists may become overly concerned with helping to achieve a certain outcome and fail to use interventions that match the patient's metacognitive capacity. While MERIT is concerned with specific outcomes, it calls for careful consideration of the patient's agenda, whether readily apparent or not, and the complexity of the psychological problems he faces. It behooves the clinician to be mindful of how directing attention toward immediate problems can be a means of avoiding reflection. That being said, crisis intervention may be needed and action taken without regard for patients' metacognitive capacity (e.g., hospitalization during a period of risk for suicide). However, once the crisis has passed, it should become the subject for reflection.

A second common challenge for therapists can emerge when they feel they have finally come to an understanding of something about the patient and feel moved to share it immediately and unidirectionally. Connections between what patients think or feel may suddenly emerge in the clinician's mind that are exhilarating in their clarity. However, the urge to quickly stitch together insights may lead to making interventions at a metacognitive level that exceeds the patient's current capacity. Recall, only until patients are at S5 (having capacity for fallibility) are they capable of perceiving how things fit together in a narrative episode or link across episodes. As a result, interventions should always be tailored to the patient's current capacity for understanding.

Third, some patients' agendas may lead them to represent themselves as having a greater capacity for metacognition than they actually possess. It is not uncommon for patients to want therapists to see them as intelligent and may attempt to discuss the fallibility of their experiences to impress the therapist with how even-minded they are. Additionally, some patients who have been in supportive therapy for years may be well-versed in "psychological jargon" and may appear to be able to put together much more than they actually can. In these situations, therapist inquiry is needed to understand whether the patient is actually capable of recognizing different nuanced emotional experiences when they are discussing the ways in which their thoughts are fallible. As emphasized throughout this book, distinguishing actual metacognitive activities from ones that mimic them is a complex but necessary task for all MERIT therapists.

Stimulating Awareness of the Other (O)

Patients Not Capable of O1

As with patients not capable of S1, patients not capable of O1 represent the most disabled. They may act without any awareness of others as unique beings, appear to be in an autistic state and simply ignore the therapist's presence, or offer seemingly irrelevant comments. Just as interventions for S0 involve simply noticing the patient's movement or speech acts, interventions that stimulate the most basic aspects of O might include noticing that the patient is aware of the therapist's presence or that the patient has (or has not) responded to the therapist's words. Here, the overarching goal is to establish a shared understanding that the patient is avoiding the experience of another person which opens the possibility that there exists another person who might have some kind of internal experience himself (O1). Table 13.2 presents a summary of the typical interventions and outcomes for differing levels of the O scale.

Table 13.2 Characteristic Outcomes and Interventions for Awareness of Others (O)

Level	*Outcome*	*Interventions*
O1	Patients realize others have mental experiences.	• *An idea came to her that . . .* • *You think he could see that . . .*
O2	Patients realize that others have their mental experiences that are their own.	• *You think she had a thought that . . .* • *He formed the idea that . . .*
O3	Patients can understand others have recent and distal memories and immediate experiences as well as unique thoughts and subjective experiences.	• *She recalled . . .* • *He planned . . .* • *She chose not to . . .* • *He was imagining . . .*
O4	Patients can understand that the life events and/or experiences in the moment of others are imbued with different emotions.	• *Now she was feeling . . .* • *His feelings have changed.* • *He has two different feelings about . . .*
O5	Patients can understand others' intentions and wishes as discernable from their verbal and non-verbal communications.	• *You think when person x says y with that expression on her face, she means z.* • *You can see how when person x feels y he tends to want z from you.*
O6, O7	Patients can express complete and rich descriptions of others in single events, across different events, and across the span of their life respectively.	• *His thoughts and feelings were connected when . . .* • *Her thoughts were connected to her feeling both times . . .* • *Across his life his thoughts and feelings have . . . because of . . .*

Patients Capable of O1 and O2

Patients capable of O1 and O2 are uncertain whether others have mental activities and, if so, whether those activities uniquely belong to the other person. Interventions at O1 and O2 should seek to locate mental events in the minds of other people. As an illustration, a patient reported that on his morning bus trip he saw his fellow passengers carrying out the wishes of Satan to persecute him. The therapist, assessing the patient as functioning at O1, responded: "You noticed there were other people taking the bus to the mall. You saw others looking at you because of the influence of the devil." For the patient assessed at O2 who reported others on the bus had their own private reasons for having malicious intent toward him, the therapist might alternatively say: "You can see others looking at you and having their own thoughts about you." Since the patient is not able to represent others in complex ways, there is no point in exploring the adequacy of ideas he is forming about others. In either case, the therapist seeks to highlight how the patient is thinking about and forming representations of others. These interventions invite patients to form an idea of how they are seeing another person that might be shared with the therapist. They also serve to acknowledge that the patient has ideas about other people and those ideas might be jointly understood by the therapist and patient.

Reflection about patients' thoughts about others can also be made on the basis of the representations the patient forms of the therapist, which also has the advantage of reflecting upon something occurring in the moment. For instance, if a patient at O1 or O2 says that people on the bus were following the wishes of Satan, a therapist might ask: "What do you imagine is in my mind as you talk about this?" This intervention serves to stimulate patients to reflect upon what they are thinking about the therapist and to notice that the patient *is* representing other people.

As an illustration, consider the patient who was recently released from a psychiatric hospital after making violent threats. The patient expressed little concern about his behavior after discharge and simply presented it as something that was in the past. With no reference to the possibility others might have experienced this in their own way, the therapist's intervention was to stimulate the patient to wonder if the therapist may have had her own personal reactions to this event. The intent of these discussions is not to empathize with, soothe, or punish the patient. Rather, the goal is to help him to recognize that the therapist has her own thoughts. Interestingly, the patient's initial response was to say that he did not think the therapist had any thoughts about him because she had been "trained not to" but was eventually able to discuss his perceptions of her related to the hospitalization.

Evidence of growth in metacognitive capacities at these levels can be seen in patients' descriptions of life events as they increasingly mention specific others. Concurrently, their speech might also reflect fewer comments about people in general who are not remarkably distinct from one another.

Patients Capable of O3

For patients who are capable of O3, interventions should focus on patients thinking about the different cognitive operations that others have. This can include reflections as simple as: "You notice person x had a memory," "You are aware that person x is forming a plan to y," or "I wonder if you have an idea about how person x might remember." The intent is for patients to become increasingly able to notice how they are seeing others' cognitive operations. For example, if in talking about a family picnic the patient describes the different things he thought might be happening in the minds of his siblings, those perceived thoughts might be emphasized by the therapist.

As in the case of interventions at S3, therapist comments should be about patients' experience in either a specific episode or in the moment with the therapist. If the intervention relates to the therapist, the therapist should stimulate the patient to think about a cognitive operation she is experiencing such as: "You realize I have memories of my childhood, too." Interventions should always be about specific individuals or meaningful units of people (e.g., the patient's sister or a group of uncles, but not large amorphous group like Republicans or impoverished farmers). As in the case of S, MERIT therapists should not prescribe abstract or didactic exercises, which ask patients to call to mind an imaginary situation in which imagined persons may have thought certain things. Instead reflections about others should emerge in an organic and natural manner and be driven by the patient's curiosity and their agenda.

Evidence of progress at this level can be seen in increasing verbalizations about others having unique and differentiated mental activities. This might lead to the production of narratives that not only frequently mention a growing cast of participants but also people who are increasingly distinct from one another.

Patients Capable of O4

Interventions for patients at O4 should stimulate their ability to recognize and distinguish the different emotions they perceive that others are experiencing. Reflections might be offered which are as simple as: "You notice that person x was feeling y," "You have the idea that person x was having a strong emotion when y," or "You didn't mention anything about what person x might have felt when z happened." The goal here is not attainment of knowledge of a specific state but developing an awareness of the subjective experience of the other's emotions. The accuracy of an intervention is less important than what it provokes. So, for example, if a patient responds, "No, you're wrong. It's more like I think person x felt y and z," the therapist's intervention would still be judged successful.

Looking to interventions that stimulate patient thoughts about the therapist, clinicians might merely comment on the patient's curiosity about the therapist's thoughts or respond when the patient queries whether the therapist is experiencing a certain emotion. As an illustration, consider the patient who asks: "Are you angry?" or "Are you feeling bored?" While this might be used as an opportunity to reassure the patient by saying, "I'm not angry with you," it also affords the opening to notice the patient's attempt at a particular form of metacognition. For instance, the therapist might say: "You are thinking about my feelings" or "When you think about my emotions, you can only see negative ones." Certainly, if the patient accurately perceived that the therapist is indeed tired, it might be helpful to acknowledge this. However, the intent is not to help the patient to correctly discern the therapist's emotional or physical states but to highlight the act of thinking about it and how the process of thinking can be considered in its own right.

Evidence of progress at this level includes increasingly nuanced portraits of others not only experiencing thoughts but also emotions within life narratives. In these richer narratives, there may also be evidence of not only the patient reacting to a given episode but also how the other actors are seen in an increasingly differentiated way, providing a new depth and multidimensionality.

Patients Capable of O5

For patients at O5, interventions should stimulate thinking about how others are communicating their intentions to the patient. This might appear in reflections such as: "You can recognize that your husband was trying to get you to forgive him" or "Your sister did x because she wanted you to offer to comfort her." Here, the goal is to stimulate reflection about the experience of another person wanting the patient to do or think something. The therapist's task is to emphasize reflection, not just about the mental states of the other but also what they may be seeking to communicate to the patient and others. This can also be applied to the interpersonal dynamics within the session. For example, the patient and therapist might jointly reflect on the patient's conclusion about what the therapist might want her to do and why.

Growth in this level might be marked by patient narratives that are not only populated by an increasing number of distinct people but also how the events described in narratives are driven by the needs of multiple people. This growth can be seen not only in the presence of an increasing number of people but also in how they are attempting to influence the things that are happening.

Patients Capable of O6 and O7

For patients assessed as capable of O6 and O7, interventions should be offered which stimulate integrated representations of others within single narrative episodes and across narrative episodes, respectively. This may involve joint and compassionate reflection about the lives and experiences of others in the patient's life including their thoughts, needs, and wishes. As is the case with lower levels of O and all the levels of S, the goal is not to assist patients to form "correct" perceptions but to foster the ability to think about themselves as thinking about others and to think about the ideas that others have formed and are forming.

Evidence of progress in these levels might be seen in the production of personal narratives in which there are multiple protagonists or main characters, each motivated by their own personal histories and experiences. It might also be evidenced in the development of a non-judgmental account grounded in the realization of others' limitations that in turn may lead to the development of new forms of compassion and the potential for sustained connections with others.

Common Challenges in Making O Interventions

As in the case with S, one common challenge therapists experience when seeking to implement Element 7 is exploring content which distracts from the process of in-session assessment of and focus on O. This often occurs when the patient offers a rather implausible or excessively negative account of another person or event which redirects the therapist to focus on correcting that perception before moving on. This might include comments about the therapist that she feels compelled to correct. Seeking to dispel such thoughts may lead to discussions that do not stimulate the patient's metacognitive capacity at the optimal level. Additionally, even when it seems appropriate for the clinician to directly address the content of a negative thought, there should also be reflection about that negative thought as an experience in the mind of the patient.

A second challenge for clinicians is the risk of becoming distracted by thinking about the psychology and lives of other people who appear in the patient's narratives and losing focus on the patient himself. For example, a therapist's curiosity may lead her to spend excessive time exploring and wondering about the patient's partner's faults and virtues while neglecting to engage in joint reflection with the patient about the emerging ideas he has about others.

A third potential challenge is therapists' failing to appreciate how some patients may avoid exploration of other people's feelings because of the inherent threats to self-esteem this may pose. For instance, a patient might refuse to consider his wife's point of view for fear of being viewed as at fault for a recent conflict and having hurt her feelings. In such cases, it may be helpful to both notice the lack of consideration of his wife's emotions and also to make a guess about the underlying reasons (e.g., avoiding these thoughts protects the patient from blame). This type of intervention allows for the observation that the patient is capable of perceiving the other person's emotions but is motivated not to do so for reasons that are understandable.

MERIT-TAS Element 7

The MERIT Therapist Adherence Scale (MERIT-TAS) Element 7 scale can be found in Table 13.3. As noted in the table, satisfactory adherence to this element requires frequent stimulation of patients to think about either themselves

Table 13.3 MERIT-TAS Element 7

Score	*Level of Adherence*	*Therapist Behavior*
0	Absent	Failure to stimulate S or O at the appropriate level using the MERIT-IF
1	Marginal	Singular or infrequent attempts to stimulate S or O generally at the appropriate level using the MERIT-IF
2	Satisfactory	Frequent attempts across the course of the session to stimulate S or O more often than not at the appropriate level using the MERIT-IF
3	Optimal	Frequent attempts across the course of the session to stimulate S or O consistently at the appropriate level using the MERIT-IF

or others, which are more often than not at the appropriate metacognitive level. Optimal levels of adherence require that not only are there frequent attempts to stimulate either S or O but also that those efforts are consistent and, with few to no exceptions, at the appropriate metacognitive level. Of note, both S and O do not need to be stimulated within a given session for there to be satisfactory or optimal adherence.

14 Element 8

Stimulating Mastery (M)

Just as Element 7 asks that S and O be stimulated at an optimal level consistent with patients' current metacognitive capacities, Element 8 requires that M also be stimulated at an appropriate level. This requires therapists to be continuously aware of the patient's level of metacognitive functioning throughout sessions while also providing a safe, predictable, non-judgmental, yet provocative space for the patient and therapist to think together.

Since metacognitive capacity improves when practiced at the level which is optimal for the patient, interventions that ask patients to think in ways beyond which they are capable are frequently overwhelming and counter-productive. As an illustration, if a patient is only capable of seeking support from others when she feels depressed (M4), asking her to consider changing her thinking (M6) when she is not able do so is not likely to be particularly helpful and most likely be frustrating.

Stimulating Mastery (M)

Patients Not Capable of M1

Patients who are unaware of having a psychological problem or any life challenges are rarely offered psychotherapy because it is not thought to be useful to such individuals. In contrast, MERIT simply sees this as a reflection of a very low level of Mastery and not necessarily a barrier that must be overcome before psychotherapy can begin. As it does with all patients, MERIT seeks to fully engage these individuals by stimulating them at the appropriate level of M.

Interventions at this level will often begin with therapists expressing awareness that the patient is denying distress while not attempting to invalidate that stance. Here, it may be useful for therapists to bear in mind that the patient is likely to experience the act of others opining that she "has problems" as an affront or an aggressive act. It is essential when therapists are working with these persons to wonder about the meaning of their seeming lack of awareness of distress or interpersonal difficulties. For instance, a patient who denies any psychological issues may have an agenda to not accept a label he believes will enable others to control him or compel him into treatment.

In these situations, a tension may emerge between pursuing the patient's agenda, to establish he has no significant problems, and the therapist's efforts to stimulate M, which are intended to increase awareness of a problem. The challenge is to implement this element without working at cross-purposes with any of the other elements. One approach is for therapists to first acknowledge the patient's agenda and her right to it and then move to a joint discussion about how the current state of "no distress" may be an improvement from a past emotional state. In turn, this can open the door for the therapist's curiosity about whether there have ever been problems in the patient's life, establishing a hypothetical capacity for distress. Other patients functioning at M0 might revise their agenda from one establishing that they are not suffering to one of not engaging in conversations which they find invalidating or affirm the precedence of their family's views over theirs. Alternately, for those patients who may be unaware due to neurocognitive compromise, it might be noticed: "It is hard to know if anything might be wrong, or even if some things are going better than others." The intent of all these interventions is to position patients to look at themselves.

As an illustration, a patient who denied he had any social or psychological problems was referred for psychotherapy and agreed to come to several sessions. During the initial sessions, the therapist accepted that he was not interested in her appraisal of whether he had a problem. With time, it was jointly discovered that when the patient said he was not mentally ill, he meant: "I am like everyone else." In other words, he believed that to be mentally ill meant to be different from and less valuable than others. He also came to ask, "How can I have problems if I have no thoughts about myself?"

Evidence of progress at this level includes patients reporting the potential for psychological distress or the experience of psychic pain in the past. Further, some patients may revise their agenda from one that establishes they are not in distress to not wanting to accept a label that feels degrading or that makes no sense to them.

Patients Capable of M1

For patients capable of M1, interventions should explore the distress the patient is experiencing, no matter how implausible. If the cause of the patient's difficulties is implausible, therapists should focus on the experience that cause is being offered to explain, not the cause itself, because it provides an opportunity for agreement. For example, if a patient notes radar waves are changing his brain, the therapist should explore the experience explained by the radar waves—for example, feelings of anxiety or depersonalization which can be agreed upon and built into a plausible psychological problem.

The therapist's role with patients at this level is to better understand what they believe and how those ideas were formed. Here, therapists need to remain curious and avoid the urge to challenge patients which attempts to engage them in something beyond their current metacognitive capacities. If pressed by the patient to accept a seemingly delusional explanation, the therapist might say that the belief seems improbable to him or that he does not share the patient's ironclad certainty about it at the moment. Such discussions also afford opportunities to discuss how the patient and therapist may have different ideas and explore the patient's reaction to that.

As an illustration, a patient believed radio personalities were conspiring to make him ill. The therapeutic dyad explored how distressed and consumed the patient was with this possibility as well as how it explained the devastation and emptiness he felt. The patient also described his extreme social isolation which he linked to a foul odor the persecutors had caused him to have. This led to the reflection that the patient experienced a psychological problem the therapist could think about with the patient, namely isolation and a terrible feeling about oneself.

Progress for patients at this level can typically be seen in the development of a more nuanced description of the challenges they face as well as in their explanations for them.

Patients Capable of M2

Interventions for patients at M2 should focus on thinking about their psychological problem and trying to understand their experience of it in a narrative context. The goal is not to focus on the problem's abstract aspects but to think with the patients about themselves in real life. If the problem is feeling vulnerable or detested by others, details should be elicited about how and when this started. This permits the dyad to jointly explore how the patient is positioned to respond to the dilemma, even if no response seems possible.

For example, a patient capable of M2 reported feeling vulnerable and unsafe when her co-workers were chatting in the break room over coffee. The therapist inquired about the experience and the two jointly discussed how confused and frozen the patient felt, feeling unable to look at others, and finding her only available course of action to be sitting alone in the far corner of the room. Here, the therapist avoided suggesting a solution. Not only could the patient not imagine that one was possible but that even if she were to carry out the prescribed behavior, it would feel as if it were simply being done on behalf of the therapist. Instead, the therapist empathized with the experience of feeling trapped without an exit but also noting that perhaps they could eventually find a solution together. The intent in such situations is not to identify the optimal solution but to help the patient to think about how she was thinking and acting in regard to the problem.

Evidence of progress at this level includes the production of increasingly nuanced accounts of psychosocial challenges that patients face as well as providing an explicit elucidation of the experience of not having a response. When patients become able to name the dilemmas they face, it sets the stage for the emergence of a sense of agency because distress can now be expressed and communicated in language.

Patients Capable of M3

Interventions for patients capable of M3 should stimulate them to identify in a non-judgmental environment how they are responding to the psychological and social challenges they face. While the responses of patients at this level will largely be passive, noting how the patient's agency might even be evident in avoidant responses should be highlighted as an example of the patient's taking action. For example, a therapist might say: "When you were upset, all you felt you could do was wait for your worries to go away," "When you were angry the only thing you could do was to sleep," or "It felt at that moment like if you were to try to do anything, you would only have made it worse."

Paralleling M2, the therapist's role is not to suggest better ways to respond because patients are not able to imagine there is anything else they can do but avoid. As a result, the intent is not to guide patients to be less passive but to discover ways to think about themselves in the midst of a psychological problem. Suggesting alternative actions also runs the risk of diverting focus from the process of thinking about the patient's thinking as well as assuming a hierarchical stance with patients.

Consider the patient who noted in a passive and resigned tone that he failed to sign up for courses this semester. After the details were discussed, it was determined this was in response to fears of failure and his anger with others who have been able to go on with their lives while he was continuing to struggle. The therapist wondered aloud if the patient was looking for her to suggest a more effective way to cope. After admitting he wanted her input, the therapist asked what might have happened had she suggested he sign up for classes. The patient initially appeared puzzled but then laughed and said that if the therapist had told him what to do and things turned out poorly, it would have been the therapist's fault. This led the patient to think about himself responding to a problem in a self-directed way without someone providing him with a solution. While the patient did not explicitly plan to be more active, the possibility of his being less passive was clearly available to him.

Evidence of progress at this level can be found in patients coming to view their passive and avoidant responses to psychosocial challenges as willful choices and actions that can be the subject of reflection.

Patients Capable of M4

Interventions, like those offered at M2 and M3, should discuss psychological and social problems in one or more narrative episodes with interventions that help patients to think about themselves responding to a problem by either seeking support or actively avoiding specific aspects of the situation. For example, the therapist might comment: "You felt overwhelmed and the best thing to do was to talk to x," "When you felt understood by your husband you felt relieved," or "You just decided to not talk about x and kept the conversation focused on sports to avoid conflict."

Mastery at this level might also be seen in the patient seeking support from the therapist in the moment. If this occurs, the therapist might reflect, for instance, how the patient is seeking support in order to lessen distress over a recent conflict with her partner. Instances where the patient does not seem to want therapist support should also be noticed and discussed. In doing so, the intent is not to chastise the patient for not seeking support but to highlight the behavior and encourage her to form ideas about that.

Evidence of progress at this level includes the use of responses to psychosocial challenges as willful choices and includes reaching out for support or making decisions to avoid specific aspects of the situation, both of which can be the subject of reflection. As in interventions at M3, progress is not seen in the development of explicit plans to modify behaviors but in the consideration of its possibility.

Patients Capable of M5 and M6

Interventions at these two levels of M should include reflections about the specific changes in behaviors (M5) or thoughts (M6) that patients are pursuing in response to psychological and social challenges. These discussions should position the patient as someone who has chosen to change how he acts or thinks for a certain reason. For instance, a therapist might note at M5: "You were feeling poorly and so decided to treat yourself to a special meal and then felt better" or "You made a point to exercise and get enough sleep so you wouldn't feel stressed out for your job interview." At M6, a therapist night note: "You were feeling poorly and decided to think about yourself in a different way and then felt better" or "You decided to think positive thoughts so you wouldn't feel so stressed out for your job interview."

At this and higher levels of M where patients are doing things which rely on increasingly complex types of metacognitive capacity, interventions should also reflect how patients are taking more active steps. In the case of a behavioral or cognitive change, therapists might ask, "How were you able to do that?" or "Was that difficult to do?" In instances where the patient's M level has increased over time, the therapist might contrast the patient's experience of how they are now responding in a more active fashion to life challenges than in the past.

It is important to be aware that experiencing higher levels of Mastery may have both positive and negative consequences. While the ability to take a more active stance in the face of distress can be empowering, it can also be frightening because of the heightened expectations it brings in addition to more opportunity for failure. Further, others may find this increased sense of Mastery uncomfortable simply because of unfamiliarity with taking active steps to respond to challenges rather than passively escaping or waiting for an other person to offer reassurance.

These levels of Mastery are also accompanied by greater levels of self-efficacy. This may have a bearing on the relationship with the therapist due to fears that she may start to demand more and too much of the patient. Other patients who experience gains in Mastery may fear the therapist will leave them since they are now healthier. Still others may want recognition for their accomplishments. Should any of these issues arise, they should be used as another opportunity to think with patients about responding to challenges in an agentic fashion.

Patients Capable M7, M8, and M9

At the three highest levels of M, therapists should focus on how patients are responding to psychological problems by utilizing more comprehensive understandings of themselves (M7), themselves and others (M8), or themselves and others in the context of the larger world where there is much that is not under human control (M9). Interventions for these levels of M should either reflect how the patient is using a higher order level of Mastery or simply pose the question of Mastery as appropriate to the patient's current level of metacognitive function.

Examples of reflections about the use of metacognitive knowledge at M7 include: "Given that you have decided you're the kind of person who avoids conflicts until it is too late, you made a conscious effort to mention the things to your partner that were bothering you" or "Since you see yourself as someone quick to jump to conclusions and mistrust people, you decided to ignore what seemed like an insulting comment from your brother." Examples of interventions that simply pose the question of Mastery are: "So the problem is something your partner said, and knowing yourself as you do, you are trying to decide how to manage this" and "You have that feeling again of being insulted. Knowing what you know about yourself, you are trying to decide how to handle that without ending up in the same kinds of troubles that have plagued you in the past."

Intervention at M8 focuses on the interactive nature of the patient's interpersonal world. Examples include therapist statements such as: "Given that you are the kind of person who avoids conflicts until it is too late while your partner is someone who reacts immediately, you decided to approach it quickly but thoughtfully" or "Even though you know you are overreacting to perceived slights, your partner needs you to be direct so you have decided to express your feelings cautiously after a little more time has passed."

Interventions at M9 focus on the broader contexts of the patient's world and might include: "You can understand how the conflict with your partner was a reflection of both your strong needs for reassurance and your partner's lingering resentment about the last conflict. However, there doesn't seem to be an immediate solution since conflict and repair is part of all relationships." An intervention that poses the question of Mastery at M9 might be: "There has been conflict in your relationship, and knowing yourself and your partner and also about the inevitable ebb and flow of relationships, are you trying to decide how to manage this?" Overall, as progress is made in these areas, patients come to be able to fully manage and direct their own recovery.

Common Challenges in Making M Interventions

The first common challenge therapists have in adhering to this element is the benevolent wish to help the patient solve problems. This can lead to dogged attempts to "get" patients to do or think certain things which leads to a loss of focus on the core task of helping patients to think about themselves as persons responding to problems. It also risks shifting the locus of meaning-making from a joint activity that takes place between the dyad to something which begins in the therapist's mind (e.g., finding the solution) and is later transferred to the patient (e.g., the patient accepts and enacts the therapist's solution).

The second challenge emerges when the therapist becomes overly focused on symptoms. For instance, letting positive symptoms become the focal point of discussion can readily co-opt not only the patient's agenda but also fail to see the problems that are most real or consequential to the patient. A similar challenge involves a focus on or therapist's favorite solutions or techniques. While the use of familiar techniques such as mindfulness or guided imagery may feel comforting to the patient, they can also neglect to notice or promote the patient's own unique approaches to solving her challenges.

MERIT-TAS Element 8

The MERIT Therapist Adherence Scale (MERIT-TAS) Element 8 scale can be found in Table 14.1. As noted in the table, satisfactory adherence to this element requires frequent stimulation of patients to think about Mastery which is more often than not at the appropriate metacognitive level. Optimal levels of adherence require that not only are there frequent attempts to stimulate M but also that those efforts are consistent with few to no exceptions at the appropriate metacognitive level.

Table 14.1 MERIT-TAS Element 8

Score	*Level of Adherence*	*Therapist Behavior*
0	Absent	Failure to stimulate M at the appropriate level using the MERIT-IF
1	Marginal	Singular or infrequent attempts to stimulate M generally at the appropriate level using the MERIT-IF
2	Satisfactory	Frequent attempts across the course of the session to stimulate M more often than not at the appropriate level using the MERIT-IF
3	Optimal	Frequent attempts across the course of the session to stimulate M consistently at the appropriate level using the MERIT-IF

Section III

Implementation, Clinical, and Technical Issues

15 Practical Treatment Considerations and Learning MERIT

Practical Considerations

MERIT is generally considered to be an individual office-based form of treatment though it is possible to extrapolate its principles and elements and apply them to community-based work. MERIT is typically offered once per week every week with sessions lasting 50 minutes. There is no reason sessions could not be more frequent than once per week if clinical needs dictate. Sessions can also be shorter than 50 minutes if patients request; this often occurs early in treatment when some individuals are not able to tolerate extended periods of challenging interpersonal engagement. While some patients do prefer meeting every other week, we honor those requests but typically suggest weekly contact.

Introducing and Explaining MERIT to Patients

In order to consent to any psychological treatment, patients must have a full explanation of that treatment as well as its risks and benefits. As a result, MERIT therapists have an ethical responsibility to not only provide an explanation of MERIT but also to make sure patients know what they can expect from treatment. This requires a non-theoretical and transparent discussion about how MERIT works—by helping patients to understand themselves and others in ways that can be used to create more personally meaningful and satisfying lives for themselves. In our own practice, we are comfortable telling patients that we believe recovery is possible, that it means different things to different people, and that one of the major treatment goals is to enable people to manage their own recovery.

It is essential that MERIT be explained in language that is jargon free and fully understandable by patients. Metacognition is a complex concept, and patients cannot be expected to understand this at the outset nor endure an extensive lecture before they can grasp what they are consenting to. We do not recommend that MERIT begin with extensive psychoeducation, for example. Rather, it might be explained that MERIT involves an extended discussion between the patient and therapist about "you and your life," "you and the people around you," and "how some things have gone poorly and others have gone well, both recently and in the past."

Therapists should also share that this process will involve the therapist getting to know the patient and the kinds of experiences he has had. In explaining the potential benefits, therapists can say things like, "MERIT wants to help people to get a better sense of themselves and other people in order to figure out how to have a better life" or "By helping to understand things better, MERIT tries to help people to become fully in charge of their own recovery." The risks are the same ones found in more standard therapies in that greater awareness may bring pain. Some patients are also explicitly concerned that therapy will reduce positive symptoms which they find pleasurable or reassuring in some way. In these cases, we have candidly indicated that this may be the result.

Discussion of the purpose and effects of MERIT should be responsive to the individual's concern. For example, if patients have a specific and concrete problems such as a lack of romantic relationships or what they believe are symptoms of a mental illness, therapists can suggest that treatment may help them to more effectively deal with those problems and have their needs met. For patients who state they are confused and unsure what they are looking for, therapists can say something to the effect of: "If we meet weekly and talk about you and your life, maybe we can make sense of what you are facing and help you decide what you want to do about it." For patients who have distressing or all-consuming delusions, we have suggested that "thinking together might make the distress easier to manage or help you have other thoughts in your mind."

Some of the most difficult challenges faced by therapists when introducing MERIT occur when patients have been pressured into treatment, most commonly by family members or legal authorities, but deny emotional distress. When patients have come to see us under these conditions, we have suggested: "Others have wanted you come here; maybe that was not something you asked for or wanted. Maybe, though, we can get to know one another and perhaps I can be helpful somehow." In this and similar scenarios, the intent is for the therapist and patient to agree to talk in order to see if something arises that might lead the patient to decide if she would like to continue meeting. In our experience, it is not infrequent that patients, particularly those with poor insight or significant negative symptoms, often agree to "just coming to talk" to see if it can be helpful in some way. We have often expressed faith that MERIT can genuinely help and that the patient's circumstances, no matter how dire, can be understood and a path to a satisfying life found.

Phases of Treatment

Like virtually all other models of psychotherapy, MERIT has a beginning, middle, and end phase. And like many other therapies, different processes are more prominent at different points though there are no hard and fast rules, and treatment will invariably play out somewhat differently for each patient.

It is common in the early phases of MERIT that considerable amounts of time will need to be devoted to establishing a therapeutic relationship. Because difficult work may lie ahead, building and maintaining rapport is vital for success. Issues that frequently arise often center on whether the patient is willing to be known. As noted earlier, intersubjectivity is often experienced as a threat by persons with psychosis, and it often requires the therapist to directly state that patients are ultimately in control of what they are willing to share and can decide when they will allow the therapist to know them. Therapists also need to carefully manage this process because patients who feel isolated and confused may not necessarily welcome the experience of becoming known by the other. Indeed, offers of compassion may be seen as threatening. As mentioned earlier, some patients may only be able to tolerate shorter sessions of 30 or even 15 minutes. In a recent case, a patient who could initially sit for no longer than five minutes when treatment started soon became able to stay for the full 50 minutes and eventually asked for a second visit each week after a year of treatment.

In the middle phases, it is expected that a richer sense of the patient's personal history, including events both linked with and unrelated to the onset and progression of mental illness, will emerge. Additionally, the greater sense of agency that comes with increased understanding of self and others may be experienced as alien and challenging by some. However, a richer degree of self-coherence allows patients to take greater charge of their own recovery and find a path to wellness.

There may be interruptions in treatment during this middle phase. Patients may suddenly announce, for example, that they need a "break," only to return weeks or months later. Others may simply stop appearing for several consecutive sessions. In either case, patients should be encouraged but never pressured to return, and these breaks jointly understood with the patient. Breaks in treatment can sometimes be linked to a wish to establish that the patient has control over whether she attends or not. Other times, they are caused by surprise at the pain that emerges with awareness. For instance, we have had patients report that they started treatment intending to be understood but did not anticipate how difficult it would prove to be, leading them to request some time away. The clinical task is to ponder what led the patient to want to decide to withdraw. This should not have a punitive quality but rather be taken as an opportunity for reflection.

The final stage of treatment is often marked by the patient's growing sense of having accomplished what she sought to obtain. This can include having achieved specific goals, substantially improved levels of metacognition, or what may be maximally possible for her.

Here, it is important to recognize that there are likely ceiling effects for some patients, and not all patients should be expected to reach the highest levels of functioning. The move toward termination can also emerge abruptly as patients suddenly realize that they have obtained what they need in order to take charge of their lives or more gradually as there comes the slow realization they are no longer in need of MERIT.

Termination in MERIT is similar to termination in most forms of psychotherapy. As the end of treatment approaches, there should be a review of the therapy process including how challenging moments emerged and how they were overcome. It also should be clearly established how clinical gains were the result of the patient's acting as an agent. Following the spirit of all that has been written in this manual, this discussion should be non-hierarchical and honest. If there is sadness about the relationship ending, as there will most often be, it should be noted and acknowledged by both therapist and patient. If the therapist thinks more time in treatment would be helpful for the patient, this should be noted too, but not in a way that criticizes the patient or hijacks the decision-making process. Alternatively, some patients may need permission to terminate, fearing that their wish to discontinue therapy might be seen as a sign of disrespect by someone who has helped and stood by them, an issue which again should be discussed as part of the termination process.

Length of Treatment and Rate of Change

The length of treatment is likely to vary considerably given patients' interests, goals, and challenges as well as the clinical resources that are available. Empirically, case work exists that suggests gains can occur as early as 12 weeks for some while for others significant gains do not appear until after a period of a year and a half. For the purposes of clinical trials, we suggest that therapy be offered for no less than 26 sessions. While some patients may achieve meaningful benefit before this time, most will require significant time to develop trust in the clinician and recoup capacities that many have not used in months or years, if ever.

In our experience, persons with longer periods of illness, more severe histories of trauma, higher levels of self-stigma or more severe impairments in neurocognitive function may require longer periods of treatment, perhaps in parallel with how physical therapy may take longer if an injury is more severe. That being said, the severity of metacognitive deficits is not always a good predictor of treatment length. On the one hand, some patients with more severe deficits may require significant time to progress and require longer treatment. On the other, some more severely impaired patients may obtain maximal benefit from treatment relatively quickly and feel they are ready to conclude therapy earlier than other less impaired individuals.

While metacognitive capacity tends to evolve slowly within MERIT, there are times when it may either improve abruptly or develop much less rapidly than expected and sometimes in ways that cannot be fully anticipated. There are patients who may struggle for extended periods to form more integrated ideas of themselves and others without success, despite the most careful interventions. There may also be declines or gains followed by plateaus. It is not uncommon for plateaus or periods of decline to be associated with pain that has emerged from greater levels of awareness. And these periods of gain and losses can happen between and within sessions. Returning to the metaphor of physical therapy, engaging in acts of metacognition may be painful.

Having formed a meaningful connection to another person in therapy may accentuate a patient's awareness of the lack of connections throughout his life. Patients may respond to this by pulling back from interventions that seek to stimulate metacognition, resisting being known by the therapist, or being reluctant to either provide narrative episodes or reflect on internal states. Therapists should respect these forms of self-protection and not try to "force" the patient to engage in narrative. Instead, it is best for the therapist to simply make note of what is taking place with remarks such as: "You don't want me to know you today," while keeping in mind that the most significant understandings will often emerge from uncertainty.

Treatment Adherence and Fidelity

In addition to supervision, therapists should assess their adherence to the MERIT protocol after each session using the MERIT Therapist Adherence Scale (MERIT-TAS; see Appendix II). The MERIT-TAS can also be completed by supervisors or raters who have reviewed a complete transcript of the session. A session will be considered to successfully adhere to MERIT if there are no items are scored a "0" ("absent") or if there are no more than two elements are scored as a "1" ("marginal") during a session. By tracking MERIT-IF scores across sessions, therapists can graph changes over time and detect trends and patterns in the treatment.

Learning MERIT: Supervision and Therapist Experiences

MERIT requires not only a strong understanding of the basics of psychotherapy and specific training in MERIT but also ongoing supervision from supervisors experienced in providing MERIT. We prefer group supervision so trainees of all levels, including more experienced therapists, can learn from each other and work as a group to solve the complex issues which arise in this kind of work. Group supervision also allows for both supervisor and peer support. The use of session-by-session reviews as well as audiotapes and typed transcripts are essential in this process. We also encourage looking to both classic psychotherapy texts as well as contemporary empirical work in the area in addition to the humanities (e.g., novels, movies, and poetry) to make sense of therapists' experiences of learning MERIT (cf. Leonhardt, Hamm, Fogley et al., 2015). Our supervisory approach is to foster therapist creativity by helping supervisees to develop multiple working hypotheses about what is happening in therapy sessions while maintaining fidelity to the structure of the MERIT model. Our intent is that supervision should be respectful but challenging, stimulating the kinds of metacognitive processes within the minds of therapists that we hope to foster in the psychotherapy they are offering patients. More information on MERIT training opportunities and clinical supervision is available from the MERIT Institute (www.meritinstitute.org).

While MERIT changes the lives of patients, it can also change the lives of therapists. It opens their awareness to many different kinds of internal experiences that can impact how they understand themselves. These reactions will vary according to therapists' own unique constellations of experience and emotion, life goals, and reactions when encountering others in emotional pain. However, there are several challenges that are commonly seen.

The first is discomfort with the uncertainty present at the outset of every session. Concretely, the therapy room door closes, the patient and therapist are seated, and the conversation has to begin. When patients feel confused and unsure what to say, as often occurs in persons with serious mental illness, therapists naturally wonder about what is going to take place. One common worry is that nothing will happen. Since there is no way to know what will occur in advance, therapists must tolerate uncertainty in that moment. This experience may be aversive and run counter to the ways therapists have previously felt when delivering treatment using highly scripted interventions. Since many therapists chose their profession in order to bring comfort to others, feelings of inadequacy can develop quickly if clinicians start feeling confused as soon as the session starts. Supervision should both normalize this experience and frame it as an unavoidable necessity of this type of work. Such experiences may also offer therapists the opportunity to become more comfortable with a broader range of their own internal experiences and to eventually make use of them within MERIT.

A second common reaction among therapists is guilt for not "fixing" patient problems or anxiety that there is something that they should be doing in addition to attempting to understand the patient. This may expose a lingering doubt on the part of therapists that human understanding can actually offer something essential in the face of deep distress. It may also stir memories of times when the therapist did not feel understood or did not understand someone well enough. Sitting with profound pain may be quite uncomfortable for the therapist, and instead of allowing its expression, a therapist might thwart the growth that is emerging by trying to soothe that patient and thereby manage his own anxiety. It may also unearth thoughts about the limits to which people can actually come to understand one another. Supervision can serve to both normalize these feelings and explore therapists' resistance to feeling vulnerable when they are not able to fully understand a patient or what is taking place.

A third, more complex reaction to offering MERIT may lie in the therapist's experience of emotional distress in fully appreciating the degree of destruction that has been wrought in the patient's life. Therapists may be profoundly alarmed when they realize how completely isolated the patient is, how traumatic the experience of psychosis has been, or how the inhumanity of previous psychiatric treatment has had a lasting impact. Clinicians may also recoil as they come to understand the trauma patients have experienced or how much distance has to be traversed for the patient to move from where they are now to a place where a reasonable quality of life may be achieved.

While clearly difficult issues, supervision may help therapists to accept how profoundly unhappy and alone many people actually are, and how trauma is not as rare as we may often believe. Supervision can also help clinicians to become more comfortable in exploring the patient's pain by encouraging them to reflect openly about times in their lives when they have had similar experiences. At other times, the underlying problem may lie in the therapist's resistance to the experience of his own pain. If so, supervision may need to examine the common dynamic of therapists being fearful that their personal experience of emotional distress is a sign of ill health and therefore resist acknowledging being anything but happy. Since MERIT entails entering into a close therapeutic relationship with a patient which is fundamentally intersubjective, it is not surprising that it will frequently have a major impact upon therapists and have the potential to trigger psychological growth.

A fourth common reaction to therapists' growing knowledge of the experience of psychosis is discovering aspects of the human condition that they had either not previously noticed or had warded off. This could include seeing how all human beings are collectives of many complementary, opposing, and unrelated elements and how often our beliefs about ourselves as possessing a solid unwavering identity are in part illusory. As health emerges and patients become more complex and multifaceted being with complimentary and contradictory elements, therapists may be challenged to think about themselves and others in new and more complicated ways. Dramatic movements toward health may, for example, surprise and unsettle some therapists. Recovery may also unearth a therapist's stigmatizing views of the potential of persons with serious mental illness to recover. Here we offer no solution to this dilemma, only direction that in supervision these and other matters should be subject to continuous open reflection.

Avoiding Therapist Demoralization

A final concern we will address concerns therapist demoralization, sometimes called burnout or compassion fatigue (e.g., Adams et al., 2006). We do not believe that mutual reflection and joint confrontation of pain is necessarily fatiguing. What can be tiring and exhausting is therapists' denial of their own experiences, either their own true reactions to patients or of what MERIT has revealed to therapists about themselves. Therapists who find themselves in a position of pretending, to themselves and others, for example, that they only have warm and kind feelings toward all patients or that they are without unhealthy or contradictory aspects of their personalities are likely to experience prolonged periods of exhaustion and might describe themselves as "burned out." Just as bad are situations in which therapists feel a need to masquerade as having all the answers and not be confused by vagaries and impossible complexities of the human condition, which can only leave therapists feeling as if they are pretenders and their activities ultimately meaningless.

This brings up a related struggle for many who practice psychotherapy: the fear that one is a pretender. MERIT regards the fear of being a pretender as potentially healthy as well as a potential guard against actually becoming a pretender. MERIT requires openness, vulnerability and honesty about our experience and limitations as human beings. Here, such fears of being a pretender are potentially healthy because they bring the experiences of openness, vulnerability, and honesty about experience, and our limitations as human beings to awareness. Striving to be true to those practices sets the stage for the practices of MERIT to be enduringly engaging and part of an evolving professional life. This can help to ensure the work will remain fulfilling and meaningful.

Therapist Self-Disclosure

It is natural for patients in psychotherapy to wonder about the personality and life of the therapist, and patients often report that therapist self-disclosure is helpful. MERIT asks that therapists be open in their relationships with patients, so using self-disclosure may be an appropriate aspect of this. However, as in all forms of therapy, therapist self-disclosure should be done solely for the patient's benefit and never to fulfill the therapist's own personal desires and needs.

Self-disclosure can be quite effective when it scaffolds the creation of a narrative episode, facilitates the formulation of a psychological problem, or when it models reflectivity. For instance, the patient who feels overwhelmed by paranoid feelings that vast numbers of people hate him might find it helpful to learn that the therapist has at times felt despised by others and has been unsettled by that feeling. The disenfranchised patient might find it helpful to hear about a time in a therapist's life in which she felt unconnected to others and very alone. Additionally, the therapist's sharing with a defensive patient how she was bullied in high school not only helped the patient to see he was not alone in that experience but also helped him to decide how to describe that and related experiences. In another example, a patient offered a narrative episode involving his mother's death from cancer and a recent visit to her grave. The therapist then self-disclosed something about a visit to her father's grave. The patient then used that to sort how his experience was alike and different from the therapist's, making progress in the moment by moving from S3 to S4.

In MERIT, once patients know they can use the therapist's experience to make sense of their own, they will often begin to ask about it. For instance, a patient asked about the therapist's relationships with his siblings and how they manage their conflicts in order to better think about his own sibling disagreements. Since it appeared that the patient wanted this information to think about himself, and not for voyeuristic or other inappropriate reasons, the therapist asked for a little more direction about what kind of scenario the patient wanted to learn about. Knowing that the therapist was an art lover, the patient asked: "What if your family does not like your tastes in art or books or politics?" In response, the therapist shared a real-life example of such a conflict that helped the patient to think about the different perspectives and emotional states of his siblings. Of note, and like any other intervention, the use of self-disclosure should only be done in a way that does not exceed the patient's metacognitive capacity.

Homework

At the present moment, many if not most cognitive interventions stress that the effectiveness of the treatment will be enhanced by therapists giving patients assignments or homework. These can include both exercises as well as formal worksheets on topics therapists deem essential. In MERIT, however, the bulk of the material that allows the consideration of patients' thoughts about themselves and others comes largely from what patients remember and the reflections they have about their internal experiences in the moment in the session as related to that memory. Homework, as well as directed exercises in session, may be helpful in some regard assuming it is directed jointly by patients; however, such interventions are less likely on their own to be effective ways of developing a shared understanding of how patients are thinking. They risk, for example, being too abstract, authoritarian, or impersonal.

Additionally, while patients may draw general conclusions from homework or exercises, it is difficult to know how those are tied to lived experience. For example, patients may learn something about what thoughts are in their mind from a thought record without necessarily being able to use that information to form an image of themselves in the flow of regular life. Moreover, since these kinds of therapist activities direct patients' thoughts, they risk taking charge of the meaning-making process. As such, they should not be the primary source of material for consideration in therapy. On the other hand, if patients bring self-generated writings to discuss or wish to have homework assignments, these may generate meaningful reflections. In the spirit of MERIT, however, the meaning behind this should be explored. For instance, in cases where it appears that the patient is seeking homework to position the therapist as a kind of powerful voice of reason or as part of a generally helpless stance, the therapist should offer a reflection about this rather than placate the patient by responding to the dilemma of the moment.

16 Common Clinical Issues

In helping patients to recover from serious mental illness, it is expected MERIT therapists will encounter a number of different problems and challenges. This chapter will discuss some of the most commonly encountered.

Comorbid Substance Abuse

A high percentage of persons diagnosed with serious mental illness will have problems with substance abuse including both alcohol and drugs. Indeed, it has been suggested that in some patients this may play a causal role in the development of the disorder as well as the persistence of deficits (Alderson et al., in press). Certainly, heavy substance use is likely to be a profound barrier to the development of metacognitive capacity and should be addressed prior to beginning MERIT. For most patients who abuse substances, MERIT typically encourages harm reduction as opposed to immediate abstinence which may be unrealistic. Additionally, many patients will come to identify substance abuse as a psychological problem during treatment with a desired outcome being long-term resolution of the issue.

Other patients may not see their substance abuse as a problem. One principle activity of MERIT is inserting the mind of the therapist, sharing with patients what the clinician is thinking. In this way, therapists might reflect upon the obvious negative consequences of substance use for those patients who do not see it as an issue by wondering about the impact it has on their lives and how they understand it. Or it may be useful to explore the feeling that the patient is seeking prior to making the decision to use and what concrete effect the substance has upon him. The goal of such interventions is not to badger the patient into dealing with drug and alcohol abuse, but for the therapist to share her mind as she would about any seemingly counter-productive behavior.

Emotional Distress and Suicidality

Emotional distress is not only common in persons with prolonged psychotic disorders but is also a likely a consequence of their isolation, loss of hope, social stigma, and demoralization. Significant levels of depression and anxiety may also be part of the clinical picture in addition to the pain that may come with increased self-awareness. Exacerbations of depression and anxiety should be carefully monitored with suicide risk evaluated routinely to include assessments of risk and protective factors. There may be a link between insight and increased suicide risk (Ekinci et al., 2012), so dangerousness to self should be routinely assessed and documented for patients with risk factors for suicide or who lack protective factors. Standard and well-accepted methods of suicide prevention should also be used in the practice of MERIT.

It is also important to view expressions of suicidality as another issue for reflection. For those patients who make repeated suicide threats, there may be times when it is appropriate to wonder aloud how this interferes with joint reflection. While clinicians should obviously take suicidal ideation seriously and use all measures necessary including facilitating hospitalization if needed, it is important to leave open the possibility that suicidality may be a form of interpersonal communication and part of an agenda that extends beyond patients simply wanting to report that they intend to harm themselves.

Exacerbation of Symptoms

It is not uncommon for many persons diagnosed with serious mental illness to experience periods of symptom exacerbation, not only in terms of emotional distress but also in the form of positive, negative, or cognitive symptoms occurring more frequently or becoming more disruptive to daily life. If this becomes apparent to therapists, they should reflect this when they share their mind by inquiring if the patient has noticed this too (assuming she has not mentioned it) and whether it is a problem. Therapists should also contemplate what may have occurred to trigger the exacerbation, including events in recent sessions. For example, it may not be a coincidence that the patient appears acutely psychotic and disorganized immediately after a session in which considerable amounts of trauma were disclosed. Generating and exploring these hypotheses will assist the therapist to understand better and empathize with the patient's state.

Therapists should also continue to try to understand patients who are experiencing acute symptom exacerbations, promoting whatever reflectivity is possible in the moment. Following periods of exacerbation, it is likely the dyad will talk about those experiences in depth, what it was like for the patient, and what she makes of it. There may also be a discussion of the therapist's experience of the exacerbation. Here, it may be reassuring for patients to know the therapist was not scared or hurt by these experiences and that the relationship is still strong. If therapists feel confused about how and why there was a period of symptom exacerbation, that can also be shared along with confidence that the dyad will be able to understand it with time.

Crisis and Hospitalization

As was mentioned earlier, hospitalization may be necessary for a range of reasons including dangerousness to self or others or symptom exacerbations. Hospitalizations may also be precipitated by psychosocial crises. Therapists should strictly follow all the standards of their profession by always thoroughly ensuring patient safety and minimizing risk.

While crises should not be ignored, therapists should be open to understanding their meaning and not necessarily accept matters at face value. By exploring the crisis of a patient who wishes to be hospitalized because of a symptom exacerbation, a therapist might discover this is related to a conflict with a family member, a wish to be cared for, or a plea to be taken seriously by the institution. In such instances, a therapist using MERIT would think about this as the unearthing of the patient agenda which may or may not actually result in hospitalization.

When possible, discussions of hospitalization should be mutual. In instances in which a patient has to be involuntarily committed, that should be discussed in an open and frank manner. In our practice, we have freely shared our reasons for committing a particular patient, including fears about his safety. We have also expressed distaste in other situations for having to hospitalize a patient but again pointed out why we acted as we did. In such circumstances, it is important to allow patients to be angry with the therapist and acknowledge the need for repair and the rebuilding of trust. Indeed, conversations about the events that led up to an involuntary hospitalization, reflections about the therapist's motives, and the patient's subsequent reactions are rife with opportunities to stimulate metacognition. In this way, the post-hospitalization period can become a time for rich exploration and never viewed at face value as a failure in treatment.

Trauma History

Trauma is common in the life histories of persons with serious mental illness and often includes childhood sexual and physical abuse. Trauma history may also be a factor that precipitates psychosis as well as a risk for enduring affective instability, psychosocial deficits, and disturbances in attachment (Bebbington et al., 2004).

Trauma history may complicate formation of the therapeutic alliance because compassionate overtures on the part of therapists may be experienced as a threat or potential seduction. As a result, therapists may need to consider this if the alliance is slow to form or unusually prone to ruptures. Therapists may also need to assure patients of their safety and be sensitive to their concerns, explicit or not, of having their trust again violated. In cases where the patient appears concerned about sexual interest on the part of the clinician, it is important that the patient feel able to voice this fear and be explicitly reassured that sexual contact will not be part of the relationship.

If a history of trauma has been discovered or reported, patients should be asked if they think it is relevant and if they are comfortable discussing it. Those who are not comfortable discussing it in the moment should be reassured they can bring it up again in the future any time they choose. It is frequent that patients will eventually identify managing or resolving the consequences of trauma as a psychological problem to be addressed in MERIT. If not, and the patient is at M2 or higher, therapists can ask if living with the consequences of trauma is something the dyad should consider. That being said, therapists should not impose a focus on trauma if it is not part of the patient's agenda.

As is hopefully apparent from what has been outlined in this volume, if trauma is a focus of treatment, the integrative nature of MERIT allows for it to be addressed in any number of ways consistent with MERIT. Of note, there is some evidence that with enhanced metacognition, patients with trauma history may experience heightened levels of emotional pain (Leonhardt, Hamm, Belanger et al., 2015) and hence it might be expected that pain will need to be named and dealt with as patients with trauma histories become increasingly reflective.

Anger and Antisocial Behavior

As is the case with the general population, some persons with schizophrenia experience heightened levels of aggression or difficulties with the expression of anger. This may be related to trauma, stigma, or generally heightened levels of emotional discomfort (Ringer & Lysaker, 2014). This is not to say mental illness is a significant risk for dangerousness. Nevertheless, MERIT therapists will encounter patients for whom aggression or hostility are significant problems. Paralleling the management of suicidality, dangerousness toward others should be continuously assessed and all standard procedures followed including facilitating hospitalization and taking all appropriate steps to warn others and notify authorities. MERIT therapists also should explicitly condemn antisocial or aggressive practices as a means of self-expression or of influencing others and seek to render those behaviors ego dystonic for patients who report being comfortable with such acts.

Consistent with MERIT's principle of inserting the therapist's mind, the clinician might observe how the patients' anger makes it difficult for them to think together and makes him worry that the patient will discontinue treatment if he were to say the wrong thing. However, therapists should not discourage or impede the emergence of anger or negative feelings, either in general or directed toward the clinician. Indeed, a significant way in which MERIT promotes wellness is by helping people to name and think about troubling mental states including those linked to hostile and aggressive ideas. Indeed, aggressive and hostile wishes are part of the human condition and not necessarily problematic or pathological. Further, since many who receive MERIT have long histories of encountering trauma and social injustice, achieving wellness may require the ability to express and think about anger and rage without it leading to acting out behavior.

Similar to repeated suicide threats, it can be useful to explore how repeated threats of aggression or expressions of rage interfere with joint reflection. And while these behaviors cannot be ignored and must be taken seriously, MERIT holds the possibility of discussing these threats as a form of interpersonal communication and part of a patient's larger agenda. That being said, when patients make threats to harm others, therapists should follow all the guidelines of their profession and take all necessary precautions to ensure the safety of all.

Comorbid Medical Conditions

Many persons with serious mental illness experience comorbid non-psychiatric medical conditions. These can include diabetes, heart disease, high blood pressure, and poor dental hygiene, some of which may be related to antipsychotic medication, lifestyle, and poor compliance with medical treatment. MERIT should not ignore such conditions but collaborate with other medical professionals who are involved in the patient's care.

It is also certainly possible that non-psychiatric medical conditions and poor health practices may become a psychological problem to be discussed in MERIT. Additionally, in cases where there is an obvious lack of self-care, sharing this reflection can be a natural part of adhering to the second MERIT element of sharing the therapist's mind. Similar to substance use, the intent is not to badger patients into better self-care but for therapists to reflect upon it, just as they would with any self-destructive behavior. MERIT holds that patients have the right to make decisions about their health care. Additionally, we have often found that consultation with other health care providers may be necessary to counter the belief that people with serious mental illness should not be taken seriously if a provider holds the stigmatized belief that mental illness is synonymous with "incompetence."

Poor Insight and Medication Non-Adherence

Poor insight among persons with serious mental illness refers to unawareness or denial of what others recognize as symptoms of mental illness, the need for treatment, and the consequences of the disorder. Poor insight is a concern since it may deter some from seeking treatments that might be beneficial (Velligan et al., 2017) though others note that higher levels of insight can be a risk factor for emotional distress (Vohs et al., 2016).

As discussed earlier, poor insight is not a barrier to the provision of MERIT. Further, MERIT therapists should not confuse the growth of metacognitive capacity with the development of awareness of illness or agreement about the need for medication. Nevertheless, these are issues which may arise. For instance, therapists and patients may disagree about what causes and constitutes serious mental illness. We have our own views about this but accept that there are certainly other valid views on the subject and do not expect patients to adopt ours. Patients may decide, for example, there is no evidence that they have a brain-based disorder or offer another explanation for their problems. Here, a patient may view himself as suffering from being "too self-certain" but deny experiencing a psychosis. While MERIT is very concerned with the challenges a patient faces, it is not expected that this will result in the endorsement of any one set of beliefs about mental illness. What is more important is that the dyad agrees on an issue for joint reflection.

The same principle applies to antipsychotic medication. Many diagnosed with serious mental illness also do not believe that antipsychotic medication is necessarily helpful or even needed. The literature suggests that medication has benefits for many (Goff et al. in press) but certainly not every patient finds significant benefit, even in controlled clinical trials which are designed to optimize treatment outcome. Additionally, there is also increasing evidence that the discontinuation of antipsychotic medication at some point may be beneficial for some patients (Alvarez-Jimenez et al., 2016).

Medication adherence is not a requirement for this form of therapy. If a therapist is not credentialed to prescribe medication, then direct advice about medication is outside of their competency and patients should be directed to consult with professionals with the credentials to prescribe medication. It is important for the MERIT therapist to discuss with patients what being prescribed and taking medication means to them because one of MERIT's ultimate goals is to help patients to make better informed decisions about their health care.

Entrenched Illness Identity

Many diagnosed with serious mental illness have accepted and become comfortable with an identity defined by mental illness or perhaps its stereotypes. This is often encouraged by mainstream mental health treatment models. Additionally, self-identification as being mentally ill may even be a defining feature of community membership for some patients (e.g., the "neighborhood crazy guy"). As is the case with many of the common problems noted so far, therapists may naturally notice it as part of sharing their mind and it may also become identified as a psychological problem if the patient is at M2 or higher. A frequent experience for patients questioning the experience of having an illness-based identity is that they do not have an alternative to it. In other words, the patients may ask: "If I am not defined by mental illness, then what defines me?" In those cases, this lack of an alternative identity may also become a psychological problem.

Negative Experiences With Previous Mental Health Treatment

Many diagnosed with serious mental illness report negative if not damaging experiences with mental health treatment. This includes patients who feel they have been implicitly or explicitly told that their diagnosis of mental illness meant they were incompetent, significantly damaged, or unable to make their own decisions. Patients may also report experiences in inpatient settings where they felt they had no choice but to accept treatment or were pressured into treatment they would not have accepted had they not been in such a vulnerable position. The result is that some patients may expect therapists to engage in the same kind of behaviors or defend the behaviors of their colleagues. This may call for therapists to reassure patients that they do not hold these stigmatizing views and are willing to validate the injustice and abuse patients have previously experienced.

Outcome and Recovery

At the outset of this volume, we discussed how recovery from serious mental illness must always be self-directed. To recover, a person must manage her own recovery, clarifying the psychiatric, psychological, and social challenges she faces, and then determining how she would like to move toward health. In this, one of MERIT's primary aspirations is to help patients to improve their metacognitive capacity in order to become more able to make their own meaning of the challenges they face, decide how they want to respond to them, take action, and then reevaluate what they have done.

As a result, specific outcomes will differ between patients. For some, wellness will mean a reduction in stigma. For others, recovery will mean improvement in self-esteem, a decrease in anxiety, or a lessening of the extent to which symptoms dominate their lives. It also should be noted that while specific outcomes may be an explicit part of treatment which the therapist and patient discuss in detail, there are other situations in which patients pursue goals without sharing them with the therapist ahead of time. For example, finding a romantic partner may be something that emerges early and is a constant focus of treatment for one patient while deciding to get a car and become more socially active may be something another patient does without any discussion at all with the clinician.

MERIT is a treatment with recovery as its ultimate outcome. However, the very nature of recovery may make it impossible to know ahead of time what form it will take for a given patient. This may especially be the case for patients who have yet to form a coherent account of the challenges they face. This is why MERIT is an individualized approach that rejects any practice that has a predetermined focus on a specific issue such as symptoms. As a result, it necessitates that patient goals and outcomes be flexibly tracked and that therapists remain sensitive to how what the patient is seeking may evolve as metacognitive capacity grows over time.

17 MERIT

Past and Future

The Roots

The writer Jorge Luis Borges (1964) noted in his essay "Kafka and His Precursors" how complicated it is to construct an accurate intellectual history of any project. He described how such a history will inevitably bring together a host of contradictory sources of inspiration—ones previously unconnected to one another. MERIT is no exception. One book that MERIT is beholden to is *One Flew Over the Cuckoo's Nest* by Ken Kesey (1962). In this novel made famous by the movie of the same name, there is the character "the Chief," a mentally ill man living in a psychiatric hospital. Over the course of the novel, "the Chief" moves slowly from a state in which he can make little to no sense of the world to one in which he can understand what is happening around him and is thereby able to escape. It is a story in which someone with profound levels of madness can recover but also a novel in which the forces of psychiatric care—which should at least minimally attempt to be benevolent—were a monumental hindrance to health. A second influential work is R. D. Laing's (1978) *The Divided Self.* This book asserts that the profoundly disorganized states experienced by persons with psychosis can be understood by others and that the seemingly meaningless speech acts of such persons are rife with meaning that could be found if a person knows where to look.

These books pointed to a project which could involve helping persons with schizophrenia to recovery even though they did not speak directly to psychotherapy. Actually, each seemed to offer a view that treatment should be avoided because it only interfered with health. This brings into focus a third and most unlikely bedfellow, Harold Searles's (1965) *Collected Papers on Schizophrenia and Related Subjects.* This book attested to his experience that psychotherapy was a viable means for understanding persons with the most severe forms of mental illness and assisting them to move toward wellness. Though mostly written before Laing's and Kesey's seminal works, Searles offers the start of a solution for Kesey's Chief and the nameless protagonists in Laing's asylums.

There are other works from which MERIT has emerged. Bakhtin's (1929/1984) analysis of Dostoyevsky's novel in *Problems of Dostoyevsky's Poetics,* the novels of Dostoyevsky himself, and Nietzsche's (1886) *Beyond Good and Evil* offer a compelling view of how human beings know themselves and each other through dialogue. They highlight how we can never be a singular static and calcified being but are always changing and evolving. There also is the work of the American psychologist George Kelly (1964) who in his paper "The Language of the Hypothesis" reminds us of how terrifying it can be to become more than who we used to be and how complicated that process is as well.

There are more works to mention than space allows and a full intellectual genealogy of MERIT seems to not even be possible. We mention these few to offer, nevertheless, a glimpse of the complicated world out of which the work has and is emerging.

The Present

MERIT is in its early stages of development and only beginning to be the object of careful study. There have been two open trials of MERIT. In the first, de Jong et al. (2016) reported on offering 12 sessions of individual therapy in five different outpatient clinics by therapists in the Netherlands. Therapy sessions were an hour long and conducted in an outpatient setting. All participants were receiving pharmacotherapy and had at least moderate ratings of positive, negative, or disorganized symptoms. Nine out of 12 patients finished treatment. Effect sizes were calculated for changes from baseline to treatment end for metacognitive capacity as measured by the MAS-A. Substantial effect sizes were obtained suggesting treatment led to significant changes in metacognitive capacity.

A similar finding was obtained in Australia by Bargenquast and Schweitzer (2014). In this study, a longer form of psychotherapy was offered by supervised postgraduate psychology students. Here, 14 adult patients diagnosed with schizophrenia received metacognitively oriented psychotherapy inspired by MERIT. Of those, 11 completed a therapy course ranging in length from 11 to 26 months, and patients attended an average of 49 sessions. Treatment effects were assessed using a single-sample, pre- and post-therapy design and supplemented with a qualitative case study methodology. As in the Dutch study, analyses showed significant improvements in measures of subjective perception of recovery and clinically meaningful improvements in metacognition measured using the MAS-A.

There have also been two small randomized controlled trials of MERIT. Vohs et al. (in press) reported on 20 adults with first episode psychosis and poor insight in a trial of 24 weekly sessions of MERIT versus treatment as usual in the United States. Of the ten patients, eight completed treatment. Statistically significant gains were found in blind post-treatment ratings of insight, as well as significant improvements in a composite score capturing awareness of illness, consequences of illness, and need for treatment in the MERIT group. The authors also found no evidence of increased emotional distress or adverse events as patient insight increased.

In a second study in the Netherlands, de Jong et al. (submitted) randomized 70 adults with schizophrenia to receive a 40-week trial of MERIT versus treatment as usual. Consistent with their earlier open trial, they found significant gains in metacognition that were not accompanied by increases in emotional distress or adverse events. Taken together, these open and randomized trials suggest that MERIT is an effective treatment that is well-accepted by patients in an outpatient setting that brings meaningful clinical gains without adverse responses.

From a different perspective, Lysaker et al. (2015) conducted qualitative interviews with 12 adults who had been receiving MERIT for at least one year about their experiences of psychotherapy. Their responses were contrasted with those of 13 other adults who were receiving supportive psychotherapy for approximately the same time period. Qualitative analyses revealed all participants felt that psychotherapy led to improvements in self-esteem and the ability to think more clearly and set meaningful goals. In contrast with those receiving supportive therapy, the group receiving metacognitively oriented therapy reported feeling better able to integrate their current experiences into the larger narratives of their lives, an increased sense of agency, and growth in the ability to understand and manage pain. Overall, these studies provide evidence that metacognitively oriented psychotherapy can promote the ability to form richer and more complex ideas about oneself and others that may lead to enhanced insight. There is also no evidence of any adverse responses to treatment in any of these published reports.

Finally, over a dozen case studies (see Table 17.1) have been published exploring how MERIT can be implemented in the face of broadly differing clinical presentations while maintaining full fidelity to MERIT's core elements.

Table 17.1 MERIT Psychotherapy Case Studies

Citation	*Clinical Presentation*
Hillis, J.D., Leonhardt, B.L., Vohs, J.L., Buck, K.D., Salvatore, G., Popolo, R., Dimaggio, G., & Lysaker, P.H. (2015). Metacognitive Reflective and Insight Therapy for people in early phase of a schizophrenia spectrum disorder. *Journal of Clinical Psychology*, 71(2), 125–135.	First episode psychosis
Buck, K.D. & George, S.E. (2016). Metacognitive Reflective and Insight Therapy for a person who gained maximal levels of metacognitive capacity and was able to terminate therapy. *Journal of Contemporary Psychotherapy*, 46(4), 187–196.	Prolonged psychosis with advanced metacognitive capacity
Dubreucq, J., Delorme, C., & Roure, R. (2016). Metacognitive therapy focused on psychosocial function in psychosis. *Journal of Contemporary Psychotherapy*, 46(4), 197–206.	Prolonged psychosis with significant psychosocial dysfunction

(*Continued*)

Table 17.1 (Continued)

Citation	*Clinical Presentation*
Hamm, J.A. & Firmin, R.L. (2016). Disorganization and individual psychotherapy for schizophrenia: A case report of Metacognitive Reflection and Insight Therapy. *Journal of Contemporary Psychotherapy*, 46(4), 227–234.	Prolonged psychosis with disorganization symptoms
Leonhardt, B.L., Benson, K., George, S., Buck, K.D., Shaieb, R., & Vohs, J.L. (2016). Targeting insight in first episode psychosis: A case study of Metacognitive Reflection Insight Therapy (MERIT). *Journal of Contemporary Psychotherapy*, 46(4), 207–216.	First episode psychosis with poor insight
Van Donkersgoed, R.J., de Jong, S., & Pijnenborg, G.H.M. (2016). Metacognitive Reflection and Insight Therapy (MERIT) with a patient with persistent negative symptoms. *Journal of Contemporary Psychotherapy*, 46(4), 245–254.	Prolong psychosis with negative symptoms
Vohs, J.L. & Leonhardt, B.L. (2016). Metacognitive Reflection and Insight Therapy for borderline personality disorder: A case illustration of an individual in a long term institutional setting. *Journal of Contemporary Psychotherapy*, 46(4), 255–264.	Borderline personality disorder in a long-term institutional setting
de Jong, S., van Donkersgoed, R., Pijnenborg, G.H.M., & Lysaker, P.H. (2016). Metacognitive Reflection and Insight Therapy (MERIT) with a patient with severe symptoms of disorganization. *Journal of Clinical Psychology*, 72(2), 164–174.	Prolonged psychosis with disorganization symptoms
Arnon-Ribenfeld, N., Bloom, R., Atzil-Sloman, D., Peri, T., de Jong, S., & Hasson-Ohayon, I. (in press). *American Journal of Psychotherapy.*	Prolonged psychosis with illness identity
Buck, K.D., Vertinski, M., & Kukla, M. (in press). Metacognitive Reflective and Insight Therapy: Application to a long-term therapy case of borderline personality disorder. *American Journal of Psychotherapy.*	Borderline personality disorder in an outpatient setting
George, S. & Buck, K.D. (in press). Metacognitive Reflection and Insight Therapy for persons with severe negative symptoms of schizophrenia. *American Journal of Psychotherapy.*	Prolonged psychosis with negative symptoms
James, A., Leonhardt, B., & Buck, K.D. (in press). Metacognitive Reflection and Insight Therapy for schizophrenia: A case study of an individual with a co-occurring substance use disorder. *American Journal of Psychotherapy.*	Prolonged psychosis with substance abuse
Hillis, J.D., Bidlack, N., & Macobin, B. (in press). Metacognitive Reflection and Insight Therapy (MERIT) for persons with a schizophrenia spectrum disorder and profound history of interpersonal trauma. *American Journal of Psychotherapy.*	Prolonged psychosis with disorganization and trauma
Leonhardt, B.L., Ratliff, K., Buck, K.D. (in press). Recovery in first episode psychosis: A case study of Metacognitive Reflection and Insight Therapy (MERIT). *American Journal of Psychotherapy.*	First episode psychosis with low levels of insight and subjective recovery

These case studies further describe how MERIT can result in both objective and subjective gains that ultimately promote recovery.

The Future

Finally, there are many unanswered questions about MERIT which highlight the need for additional quantitative, qualitative, and theoretical work. It is clear that more clinical trials of MERIT as a treatment model are needed to understand the impact MERIT has on the lives of patients over time. It is also anticipated that a considerable amount of information will be learned as MERIT is used in different settings with more diverse groups of patients, including those with other forms of mental illness in addition to schizophrenia, as well as from the experiences of new MERIT therapists. Additionally, qualitative analyses of individual cases are needed along with extensive consideration of first person accounts of persons receiving MERIT in order to more completely understand the process of change that it unlocks.

Appendices

Appendix I
MERIT Intervention Framework (MERIT-IF)

Self-Reflectivity (S)

S0	Unawareness of the experience of one's own mental activities
S1	Awareness of mental activities but uncertainty whether they are one's own
S2	Awareness of mental experiences that are one's own
S3	Recognition of distinct varied cognitive operations
S4	Recognition of distinct varied emotional experiences
S5	Recognition that mental states are changing and that thoughts are subjective and fallible
S6	Recognition that hopes and wishes are potentially not aligned with reality
S7	Recognition of the mutual influence of one's thoughts, wishes, feelings, and/or behavior within a narrative episode
S8	Recognition of the mutual influence of one's thoughts, wishes, feelings, and/or behavior across and between narrative episodes
S9	Integration of multiple narratives to create a coherent and complex personal narrative

Awareness of the Other (O)

O0	Unawareness of others' experience of mental activities
O1	Awareness of others' mental activities but uncertainty whether they are their own
O2	Awareness that others' mental experiences are their own
O3	Recognition that others experience distinct varied cognitive operations
O4	Recognition that others have distinct varied emotional experiences
O5	Recognition of others' changing mental states used to make inferences about the intentions of other people
O6	Recognition of the mutual influence of another's thoughts, wishes, feelings, and/or behavior within a narrative episode
O7	Recognition of the mutual influence of thoughts, wishes, feelings, and/or behavior across narrative episodes

Decentration (D)

D0	All activities are related to the self.
D1	There are activities unrelated to the self.
D2	Events can be seen from multiple valid perspectives.
D3	Life events are often the result of complex factors that vary from person to person.

Mastery (M)

M0	No identified distress or psychological problem
M1	An implausible psychological or social problems
M2	Plausible psychological or social problems
M3	Reduction of distress through passive or grossly avoidant strategies
M4	Reduction of distress through selective avoidance or interpersonal support
M5	Active response to distress through behavioral strategies
M6	Active response to distress through altering thoughts
M7	Active response to distress through use of unique metacognitive knowledge of oneself
M8	Active response to distress through use of unique metacognitive knowledge of oneself and others
M9	Active response to distress through use of unique metacognitive knowledge of oneself, others, and the human condition

Appendix II

The MERIT Therapist Adherence Scale (MERIT-TAS)

Element 1: The agenda		
0	Absent	Failure to make the patient's agenda manifest
1	Marginal	Singular or infrequent attempts to make the agenda manifest without a significant statement emerging about the patient's agenda
2	Satisfactory	Frequent attempts to make the agenda manifest **or** a significant statement which emerges about the patient's agenda
3	Optimal	Frequent attempts to make the agenda manifest **and** a significant statement which emerges about the patient's agenda
Element 2: Insertion of the therapist's mind		
0	Absent	Failure to insert the therapist's mind
1	Marginal	Singular or infrequent attempts to insert the therapist's mind
2	Satisfactory	Frequent attempts across the course of the session to insert the therapist's mind
3	Optimal	Frequent attempts to insert the therapist's mind **and** reflection upon the impact of the therapist's mind on the patient
Element 3: Narrative episode		
0	Absent	Failure to attempt to elicit narrative episode or the lack of the emergence of a substantial narrative episode
1	Marginal	Singular or infrequent attempts to elicit a narrative episode without the emergence of a substantial narrative episode
2	Satisfactory	Frequent attempts across the course of the session to elicit a narrative episode or the emergence of a substantial narrative episode
3	Optimal	The emergence of a substantial narrative episode with nuanced exploration of relevant details
Element 4: Psychological problem		
0	Absent	Failure to attempt to elicit a psychological problem or lack of the emergence of a substantial psychological problem
1	Marginal	Singular or infrequent attempts to elicit a psychological problem without the emergence of a substantial psychological problem

(*Continued*)

(Continued)

2	Satisfactory	Frequent attempts across the course of the session to elicit a psychological problem **or** the emergence of a substantial psychological problem
3	Optimal	The emergence of a substantial psychological problem with nuanced discussion of its connection with other problems or aspects of the patient's life
Element 5: The therapeutic relationship		
0	Absent	Failure to discuss the therapeutic relationship
1	Marginal	Singular or infrequent attempts to discuss the therapeutic relationship with consideration of the therapist's role or position without the emergence of a substantial statement about the therapeutic relationship
2	Satisfactory	Frequent attempts to discuss the therapeutic relationship with consideration of the therapist's role or position or the emergence of a substantial statement about the therapeutic relationship
3	Optimal	The emergence of a substantial statement about the therapeutic relationship with consideration of the therapist's role or position, **and** the usefulness of that position
Element 6: Progress		
0	Absent	Failure to discuss progress or lack of progress within the session
1	Marginal	Discussion of the progress within the session
2	Satisfactory	Discussion of the progress within the session **with** consideration of what has caused the progress
3	Optimal	Discussion of the progress within session, its causes, **and** the effects of that progress or lack of progress on the patient (including patient reactions)
Element 7: Stimulating S and O		
0	Absent	Failure to stimulate S or O at the appropriate level using the MERIT-IF
1	Marginal	Singular or infrequent attempts to stimulate S or O generally at the appropriate level using the MERIT-IF
2	Satisfactory	Frequent attempts across the course of the session to stimulate S or O generally at the appropriate level using the MERIT-IF
3	Optimal	Frequent attempts across the course of the sessions to stimulate S or O **consistently** at the appropriate level using the MERIT-IF
Element 8: Stimulating M		
0	Absent	Failure to stimulate M at the appropriate level using the MERIT-IF
1	Marginal	Singular or infrequent attempts to stimulate M at the appropriate level using the MERIT-IF
2	Satisfactory	Frequent attempts across the course of the session to stimulate M generally at the appropriate level using the MERIT-IF
3	Optimal l	Frequent attempts across the course of the sessions to stimulate M **consistently** at the appropriate level using the MERIT-IF

MERIT-IF and MERIT-TAS rating form

Session Date PT ID **Therapist**

	S	O	D	M
9				
8				
7				
6				
5				
4				
3				
2				
1				

MERIT-TAS	*Score*
E1	
E2	
E3	
E4	
E5	
E6	
E7	
E8	

notes

References

Adams, R., Boscarino, J., & Figley, J. (2006). Compassion fatigue and psychological distress among social workers: A validation study. *American Journal of Orthopsychiatry*, 76, 103–108.

Alderson, H.L., Semple, D.M., Blayney, C., Queirazza, F., Chekuri, V., & Lawrie, S.M. (In press). Risk of transition to schizophrenia following first admission with substance-induced psychotic disorder: A population-based longitudinal cohort study. *Psychological Medicine*. DOI:10.1017/S0033291717001118

Alvarez-Jimenez, M., O'Donoghue, B., Thompson, A., Gleeson, J.F., Bendall, S., Gonzalez-Blanch, C., Killackey, E., Wunderink, L., & McGorry, P.D. (2016). Beyond clinical remission in first episode psychosis: Thoughts on antipsychotic maintenance vs. guided discontinuation in the functional recovery era. *CNS Drugs*, 30(5), 57–68.

Andreasen, N.C. (1984). *The broken brain: The biological revolution in psychiatry*. New York: Harper & Row.

Andreasen, N.C., Paradiso, S., & O'Leary, D.S. (1998). 'Cognitive dysmetria' as an integrative theory of schizophrenia: A dysfunction in cortical-subcortical-cerebellar circuitry? *Schizophrenia Bulletin*, 24(2), 203–218.

Andresen, R., Oades, L., & Caputi, P. (2003). The experience of recovery from schizophrenia: Towards an empirically validated state model. *Australian and New Zealand Journal of Psychiatry*, 37, 586–594.

Bacon, E., Danion, J.M., Kauffmann-Muller, F., & Bruant, A. (2001). Consciousness in schizophrenia: A metacognitive approach to semantic memory. *Consciousness and Cognition*, 10, 473–484.

Bakhtin, M. (1929/1984). *Problems of Dostoyevsky's poetics*. Translated by C. Emerson. Minneapolis, MN: University of Minnesota Press.

Bargenquast, R. & Schweitzer, R.D. (2014). Enhancing sense of recovery and self-reflectivity in people with schizophrenia: A pilot study of metacognitive narrative psychotherapy. *Psychology and Psychotherapy: Theory, Research and Practice*, 87(3), 338–356.

Bargenquast, R., Schweitzer, R.D., & Drake, S. (2015). Reawakening reflective capacity in the psychotherapy of schizophrenia: A case study. *Journal of Clinical Psychology*, 71(2), 136–145.

Bebbington, P.E., Bhugra, D., Brugha, T., Singleton, N., Farrell, M., Jenkins, R., Lewis, G., & Meltzer, H. (2004). Psychosis, victimization and childhood disadvantage. *British Journal of Psychiatry*, 185, 220–226.

Beebe, B., Knoblauch, S., Rustin, J., & Sorter, D. (2005). *Forms of intersubjectivity in infant research and adult treatment.* New York: Other Press.

Bellack, L. (1971). Research on ego function patterns: A progress report. In: L. Bellack & L. Loeb (Eds.), *The schizophrenic syndrome* (pp. 11–65). New York, NY: Grune and Stratton.

Bennett, H. & Wells, A. (2010). Metacognition, memory disorganization and rumination in posttraumatic stress symptoms. *Journal of Anxiety Disorders*, 24(3), 318–325.

Bleuler, E. (1950). *Dementia praecox or the group of schizophrenias.* New York: International Universities Press.

Bo, S., Abu-Akel, A., Kongerslev, M., Haahr, U.H., & Bateman, A. (2014). Mentalizing mediates the relationship between psychopathy and type of aggression in schizophrenia. *Journal of Nervous and Mental Disease*, 202(1), 55–63.

Borges, J.L. (1964). Kafka and his precursors. In *Labyrinths: Selected stories & other writings* (pp. 199–201). New York, NY: New Directions Publishing Corporations.

Brüne, M., Dimaggio, G., & Lysaker, P.H. (2011). Metacognition and social functioning in schizophrenia: Evidence, mechanisms of influence and treatment implications. *Current Psychiatry Review*, 7(3), 239–247.

Buck, K.D., Buck, B.E., Hamm, J.A., & Lysaker, P.H. (2015). Martin Buber and evidence based practice: Can the lion really lie down with the lamb. *Psychosis*, 8(2), 156–165.

Buck, K.D., McLeod, H.J., Gumley, A., Dimaggio, G., Buck, B.E., Minor, K., James, A.V., & Lysaker, P.H. (2014). Anhedonia in prolonged schizophrenia spectrum patients with relatively lower vs. higher levels of depression disorders: Associations with deficits in social cognition and metacognition. *Consciousness and Cognition*, 10(29c), 68–75.

Buck, K.D., Roe, D., Yanos, P.T., Buck, B.E., Folgey, R.L., Grant, M.L.A., Lubin, F., & Lysaker, P.H. (2013). Challenges to assisting with the recovery of personal identity and wellness for persons with serious mental illness: Considerations for mental health professionals. *Psychosis*, 5(2), 127–133.

Buck, K.D., Warman, D.M., Huddy, V., & Lysaker, P.H. (2012). The relationship of metacognition with jumping to conclusions among persons with schizophrenia spectrum disorders. *Psychopathology*, 45(5), 271–275.

Cortina, M. & Liotti, G. (2010). The intersubjective and cooperative origins of consciousness: An evolutionary-developmental approach. *Journal of the American Academy of Psychoanalysis and Dynamic Psychiatry*, 38(2), 291–314.

Davidson, L. (2003). *Living outside mental illness: Qualitative studies of recovery in schizophrenia.* New York: New York University Press.

Davidson, L., O'Connell, M., Tondora, J., Lawless, M., & Evans, A.C. (2005). Recovery in serious mental illness: A new wine or just a new bottle? *Professional Psychology Research Practice*, 36, 480–487.

Davis, L.W., Eicher, A.C., & Lysaker, P.H. (2011). Metacognition as a predictor of therapeutic alliance over 26 weeks of psychotherapy in schizophrenia. *Schizophrenia Research*, 129(1), 85–90.

Degen, K., & Nasper, E. (1996). *Return from madness: Psychotherapy with people taking the new antipsychotic medications and emerging from severe, lifelong, and disabling schizophrenia.* Northvale, NJ: Jason Aronson.

de Jong, S., van Donkersgoed, R.J.M., Aleman, A., van der Gaag, M., Wunderink, L., Arends, J., Lysaker, P.H., & Pijnenborg, G.H.M. (2016). The practical implications of metacognitive psychotherapy in psychosis: Findings from a pilot study. *Journal of Nervous and Mental Disease*, 204(9), 713–736.

de Jong, S., van Donkersgoed, R.J.M., Timmerman, M.E., aan het Rot, M., Wunderink, L., Arends, J., Van Der Gaag., M., Alemane, A., Lysaker, P.H., Pijnenborg, G.H.M. (Submitted). Metacognitive Reflection and Insight Therapy (MERIT) for patients with schizophrenia.

Dewey, J. (1922). *The middle works, 1899–1924*, Volume 14. Human Nature and Conduct. Carbondale, IL: Southern Illinois University Press.

Dimaggio, G., Montano, A., Popolo, R., & Salvatore, G. (2015). *Metacognitive interpersonal therapy for personality disorders: A treatment manual.* New York, NY: Routledge.

Dimaggio, G., Nicolò, G., Semerari, A., & Carcione, A. (2013). Investigating the personality disorder psychotherapy process: The roles of symptoms, quality of affects, emotional dysregulation, interpersonal processes, and mentalizing. *Psychotherapy Research*, 23(6), 624–632.

Dimaggio, G., Salvatore, G., Fiore, D., Carcione, A., Nicolò, G., & Semerari, A. (2012). General principles for treating personality disorder with a prominent inhibitedness trait: Towards an operationalizing integrated technique. *Journal of Personality Disorders*, 26(1), 63–83.

Dimaggio, G., Semerari, A., Carcione, A., Nicolò, G., & Procacci, M. (2007). *Psychotherapy of personality disorders: Metacognition, states of mind and interpersonal cycles.* London: Routledge.

Dimaggio, G., Vanheule, S., Lysaker, P., Carcione, A., & Nicolò, G. (2009). Impaired self-reflection in psychiatric disorders among adults: A proposal for the existence of a network of semi independent functions. *Consciousness and Cognition*, 18(3), 653–664.

Ekinci, O., Ugurlu, G.K., Albayrak, Y., Arslan, M., & Caykoylu, A. (2012). The relationship between cognitive insight, clinical insight, and depression in patients with schizophrenia. *Comprehensive Psychiatry*, 53(2), 195–200.

Firmin, R.L., Luther, L., Salyers, M., Buck, K.D., & Lysaker, P.H. (In press). The roles of metacognition and fear of negative evaluation in resisting mental illness stigma. *Israeli Journal of Psychiatry.*

Flavell, J.H. (1979). Metacognition and cognitive monitoring: A new area of cognitive-developmental inquiry. *American Psychologist*, 34, 906–911.

Fonagy, P., Bateman A., & Bateman, A. (2011). The widening scope of mentalization: A commentary. *Psychology and Psychotherapy*, 84, 98–110.

Fonagy, P., Gergely, G., & Jurist, E.L. (2004). *Affect regulation, mentalization and the development of the self.* London: Karnac Books.

Frankl, V. (1965). *Man's search for meaning.* New York: Beacon Press.

Geekie, J. (2012). The uncertainty of being: Existential aspects of the experience of psychosis. In J. Geekie, P. Randal, D. Lampshire, & J. Read (Eds.), *Experiencing psychosis: Personal and professional perspectives* (pp. 87–96). New York, NY: Routledge.

Gilbert, P. (1989). *Human nature and suffering.* Sussex, UK: Lawrence Erlbaum.

Goff, D.C., Falkai, P., Fleischhacker, W.W., Girgis, R.R., Kahn, R.M., Uchida, H., Zhao, J., & Lieberman, J.A. (In press). The long-term effects of antipsychotic medication on clinical course in schizophrenia. *American Journal of Psychiatry.*

Hamm, J.A., Buck, B.E., & Lysaker, P.H. (2015). Reconciling the ipseity-disturbance model with the presence of painful affect in schizophrenia. *Philosophy, Psychiatry and Psychology*, 22(3), 197–208.

Hamm, J.A., Buck, K.D., Leonhardt, B.L., Luther, L., & Lysaker, P.H. (In press). Self-directed recovery in schizophrenia: Attending to clients' agendas in psychotherapy. *Journal of Integrative Psychotherapy.*

Hamm, J.A., Buck, K.D., Vohs, J., Westerlund, R.J., & Lysaker, P.H. (In press). Interpersonal stance and dialogue in psychotherapy for schizophrenia: A supervisory approach. *The Clinical Supervisor.*

Hamm, J.A., Renard, S.B., Fogley, R.L., Leonhardt, B.L., Dimaggio, G., Buck, K.D., & Lysaker, P.H. (2012). Metacognition and social cognition in schizophrenia: Stability and relationship to concurrent and prospective symptom assessments. *Journal of Clinical Psychology*, 68(12), 1302–1312.

Harding, C.M., Brooks, G.W., Ashikaga, T., Strauss, J.S., & Breier, A. (1987). The Vermont longitudinal study of persons with severe mental illness, II: Long-term outcome of subjects who retrospectively met DSM-III criteria for schizophrenia. *American Journal of Psychiatry*, 144(6), 727–735.

Harrow, M., Jobe, T.H., & Faull, R.N. (2014). Does treatment of schizophrenia with antipsychotic medications eliminate or reduce psychosis? A 20-year multi-follow-up study. *Psychological Medicine*, 44(14), 3007–3016.

Hasson-Ohayon, I., Avidan, M., Mashiach-Eizenberg, M., Kravetz, S., Rozencwaig, S., Shalev, H., & Lysaker, P.H. (2015). Metacognitive and social cognition approaches to understanding the impact of schizophrenia on social quality of life. *Schizophrenia Research*, 161(2–3), 386–391.

Hasson-Ohayon, I. & Lysaker, P.H. (2017). The special challenges of psychotherapy with persons with psychosis: Intersubjective metacognitive model of agreement and shared meaning. *Clinical Psychology and Psychotherapy*, 24(2), 428–440.

James, A.V., Hasson-Ohayon, I., Vohs, J., Minor, K.S., Leonhardt, B.L., Buck, K.D., George, S., & Lysaker, P.H. (2016). Metacognition moderates the relationship between self-appraisal and social functioning in prolonged schizophrenia independent of general psychopathology. *Comprehensive Psychiatry*, 69, 62–70.

Jung, C.G. (1906/1911). *The psychology of dementia praecox.* Baltimore, MD: Nervous and Mental Disease Publishing Company.

Karon, B.P. & VandenBos, G. (1977). *Psychotherapy of schizophrenia: The treatment of choice.* New York, NY: Jason Aronson.

Kean, C.S. (2009). Silencing the self: Schizophrenia as a self-disturbance. *Schizophrenia Bulletin*, 35(6), 1034–1036.

Kelly, G. (1964). The language of the hypothesis. *The Journal of Individual Psychology*, 20, 137–152.

Kesey, K. (1962). *One flew over the cuckoo's nest.* New York: Viking Press.

Kingdon, D.G. & Turkington, D. (2008). *Cognitive therapy for schizophrenia.* New York: Guilford Press.

Koren, D., Seidman, L.J., Poyurovsky, M., Goldsmith, M., Viksman, P., Zichel, S., & Klein, E. (2004). The neuropsychological basis of insight in first-episode schizophrenia: A pilot metacognitive study. *Schizophrenia Research*, 70, 195–202.

Kraepelin, E. (1919). *Dementia praecox and paraphrenia.* Bristol England: Thoemmes Press.

Kukla, M., Lysaker, P.H., & Salyers, M. (2013). Do persons with schizophrenia who have better metacognitive capacity also have a stronger subjective experience of recovery? *Psychiatry Research*, 209(3), 381–385.

Ladegaard, N., Larsen, E.R., Videbech, P., & Lysaker, P.H. (2014). Higher-order social cognition in first-episode major depression. *Psychiatry Research*, 216(1), 37–43.

Ladegaard, N., Lysaker, P.H., Larsen, E., & Videbech, P. (2014). A comparison of capacities for social cognition and metacognition in first episode and prolonged depression. *Psychiatry Research*, 220(3), 883–889.

Laing, R.D. (1978). *The divided self.* New York, NY: Penguin Books.

Lampshire, D. (2012). The sounds of a wounded world. In J. Geekie, P. Randal, D. Lampshire, & J. Read (Eds.), *Experiencing psychosis: Personal and professional perspectives* (pp. 139–145). New York: Routledge.

Lauveng, A. (2012). When you have lost yourself, there's really not very much left. In J. Geekie, P. Randal, D. Lampshire, & J. Read (Eds.), *Experiencing psychosis: Personal and professional perspectives* (pp. 79–86). New York: Routledge.

Leonhardt, B.L., Benson, K., George, S., Buck, K.D., Shaieb, R., & Vohs, J.L. (2016). Targeting insight in first episode psychosis: A case study of Metacognitive Reflection Insight Therapy (MERIT). *Journal of Contemporary Psychotherapy*, 46(4), 207–216.

Leonhardt, B.L., Hamm, J.A., Belanger, E.A., & Lysaker, P.H. (2015). Childhood sexual abuse moderates the relationship of self-reflectivity with increased emotional distress in schizophrenia. *Psychosis*, 7(3), 195–205.

Leonhardt, B.L., Hamm, J.A., Fogley, R.L., Buck, K.D., Roe, D., & Lysaker, P.H. (2015). Allowing for psychosis to be approachable and understandable as a human experience: A role for the humanities in psychotherapy supervision. *American Journal of Psychotherapy*, 69(1), 35–51.

Leonhardt, B.L., Huling, K., Hamm, J.A., Hasson-Ohayon, I., Roe, D., Gumley, A., McLeod, H., & Lysaker, P.H. (In press). Recovery and serious mental illness: A review of current clinical and research paradigms and future directions. *Expert Review of Neurotherapeutics*

Leonhardt, B.L., Kukla, M., Chadoin, K., Belanger, E., Buck, K.D., Minor, K.S., Vohs, J.L., Hamm, J.A., & Lysaker, P.H. (In press). Emergence of psychotic content in psychotherapy: A qualitative analysis of content, process, and therapist variables. *Journal of Psychotherapy Research.*

Liotti, G. & Gilbert, P. (2011). Mentalizing, motivation, and social mentalities: Theoretical considerations and implications for psychotherapy. *Psychology and Psychotherapy*, 84(1), 9–25.

Luther, L., Firmin, R.L., Vohs, J.L., Buck, K.D., Rand, K.L., & Lysaker, P.H. (2016a). Intrinsic motivation as mediator between metacognitive deficits and impaired functioning in schizophrenia. *British Journal of Clinical Psychology*, 55(3), 332–347.

Luther, L., Firmin, R.L., Minor, K.S., Vohs, J.L., Buck, B., Buck, K.D., & Lysaker, P.H. (2016b). Metacognition deficits as a risk factor for prospective motivation deficits in schizophrenia. *Psychiatry Research*, 245, 172–178.

Lysaker, P.H., Bob, P., Pec, O., Hamm, J., Kukla, M., Vohs, J., Popolo, R., Salvatore, G., & Dimaggio, G. (2013). Synthetic metacognition as a link between brain and behavior in schizophrenia. *Translational Neuroscience*, 4(3), 368–377.

Lysaker, P.H., Buck, K.D., & Ringer, J. (2007). The recovery of metacognitive capacity in schizophrenia across thirty two months of individual psychotherapy: A case study. *Psychotherapy Research*, 17, 713–720.

Lysaker, P.H., Clements, C.A., Plascak-Hallberg, C.D., Knipscheer, S.J., & Wright, D.E. (2002). Insight and personal narratives of illness in schizophrenia. *Psychiatry*, 43(4), 319–246.

Lysaker, P.H., Davis, L.W., Eckert, G.J., Strasburger, A., Hunter, N., & Buck, K.D. (2005). Changes in narrative structure and content in schizophrenia in long term individual psychotherapy: A single case study. *Clinical Psychology and Psychotherapy*, 12, 406–416.

Lysaker, P.H., Davis, L.W., Warman, D.M., Strasburger, A., & Beattie, N. (2007). Stigma, social function and symptoms in schizophrenia and schizoaffective disorder: Associations across six months. *Psychiatry Research*, 149, 89–95.

Lysaker, P.H. & Dimaggio, G. (2014). Metacognitive capacities for reflection in schizophrenia: Implications for developing treatments. *Schizophrenia Bulletin*, 40(3), 487–491.

Lysaker, P.H., Dimaggio, G., Carcione, A., Procacci, M., Buck, K.D., Davis, L.W., & Nicolò, G. (2010). Metacognition and schizophrenia: The capacity for self-reflectivity as a predictor for prospective assessments of work performance over six months. *Schizophrenia Research*, 122(1–3), 124–130.

Lysaker, P.H., Dimaggio, G., Wicket-Curtis, A., Kukla, M., Luedtke, B.L., Vohs, J., Leonhardt, B.L., James, A.V., Buck, K.D., & Davis, L.W. (2015). Deficits in metacognitive capacity are related to subjective distress and heightened levels of hyperarousal symptoms in adults with posttraumatic stress disorder. *Journal of Trauma and Dissociation*, 26, 1–15.

Lysaker, P.H., George, S., Chadoin-Patzel, K.A., Pec, O., Bob, P., Leonhardt, B.L., Vohs, J., James, A., Wickett-Curtis, A., Buck, K.D. & Dimaggio, G. (In press). Contrasting metacognitive, social cognitive and alexithymia profiles in adults with borderline personality disorder, schizophrenia and substance use disorder. *Psychiatry Research*.

Lysaker, P.H., Gumley, A., Luedtke, B., Buck, K.D., Ringer, J.M., Olesek, K., Kukla, M., Leonhardt, B.L., Popolo, R., & Dimaggio, G. (2013). Social cognition and metacognition in schizophrenia: Evidence of their independence and linkage with outcomes. *Acta Psychiatrica Scandinavica*, 127(3), 239–247.

Lysaker, P.H., Kukla, M., Dubreucq, J., Gumley, A., McLeod, H., Buck, K.D., Vohs, J., Minor, K.M., Luther, L., Leonhardt, B.L., Belanger, E.A., Popolo, R., & Dimaggio, G. (2015). Metacognitive deficits predict future levels of negative symptoms in schizophrenia controlling for neurocognition, affect recognition, and self-expectation of goal attainment. *Schizophrenia Research*, 168(1–2), 267–272.

Lysaker, P.H., Leonhardt, B.L., Brüne, M., Buck, K.D., James, A., Vohs, J., Francis, M., Hamm, J., Salvatore, G., Ringer, J.M., & Dimaggio, G. (2014). Capacities for theory of mind, metacognition, and neurocognitive function as independently related to emotional recognition in schizophrenia. *Psychiatry Research*, 219(1), 79–85.

Lysaker, P.H. & Lysaker, J.T. (2010). Schizophrenia and alterations in self-experience: A comparison of six perspectives. *Schizophrenia Bulletin*, 36(2), 331–340.

Lysaker, P.H., McCormick, B.P., Snethen, G., Buck, K.D., Hamm, J.A., Grant, M.L.A., Nicolò, G., & Dimaggio, G. (2011). Metacognition and social function in schizophrenia: Associations of mastery with functional skills competence. *Schizophrenia Research*, 131(1–3), 214–218.

Lysaker, P.H. & Roe, D. (2016). Integrative psychotherapy for schizophrenia: Its potential for a central role in recovery oriented treatment. *Journal of Clinical Psychology*, 72(2), 117–122.

Lysaker, P.H., Vohs, J.L., Ballard, R., Fogley, R., Salvatore, G., Popolo, R., & Dimaggio, G. (2013). Metacognition, self reflection and recovery in schizophrenia: Review of the literature. *Future Neurology*, 8(1), 103–115.

Lysaker, P.H., Vohs, J.L., Hamm, J.A., Kukla, M., Minor, K.S., de Jong, S., Donkersgoed, R., Pijnenborg, M., Kent, J.S., Matthews, S.C., Ringer, J.M., Leonhardt, B.L., Francis, M.M., Buck, K.D., & Dimaggio, G. (2014). Deficits in metacognitive capacity distinguish patients with schizophrenia from those with prolonged medical adversity. *Journal of Psychiatric Research*, 55, 126–132.

Main, M. (1991). Metacognitive knowledge, metacognitive monitoring, and singular (coherent) vs. multiple (incoherent) models of attachment: Findings and directions for future research. In P. Harris, J. Stevenson-Hinde, & C. Parkes (Eds.), *Attachment across the life cycle* (pp. 127–159). New York, NY: Routledge.

Markowitz, F.E. (1998). The effects of stigma on the psychological well-being and life satisfaction of persons with mental illness. *Journal of Health and Social Behavior*, 39, 335–347.

Martin, J.K., Pescosolido, B.A., & Tuch, S.A. (2000). Of fear and loathing: The role of disturbing behavior, labels and causal attributions in shaping public attitudes toward persons with mental illness. *Journal of Health and Social Behavior*, 41, 208–223.

Massé, M., & Lecomte, T. (2015). Metacognitive profiles in individuals with a first episode of psychosis and their relation to social functioning and perceived social support. *Schizophrenia Research*, 166(1–3), 60–64.

May, R. (1958). The contributions of existential psychotherapy. In R. May, E. Angel, & H. Ellenberger (Eds.), *Existence; a new dimension in psychiatry and psychology* (pp. 37–91). Oxford, UK: Basic Books.

McLeod, H.J., Gumley, A.I., MacBeth, A., Schwannauer, M., & Lysaker, P.H. (2014). Metacognitive functioning predicts positive and negative symptoms over 12 months in first episode psychosis. *Journal of Psychiatric Research*, 54, 109–115.

Moritz, S., Woodward, T.S., Burlon, M., Braus, D., & Andresen, B. (2007). Attributional style in schizophrenia: Evidence for a decreased sense of self-causation in currently paranoid patients. *Cognitive Therapy and Research*, 31, 371–383.

Mueser, K.T. & Berenbaum, H. (1990). Psychodynamic treatment for schizophrenia: Is there a future? *Psychological Medicine*, 20, 253–262.

Nabors, L.M., Yanos, P.T., Roe, D., Hasson-Ohayon, I., Leonhardt, B.L., Buck, K.D., & Lysaker, P.H. (2014). Stereotype endorsement, metacognitive capacity, and self-esteem as predictors of stigma resistance in persons with schizophrenia. *Comprehensive Psychiatry*, 55(4), 792–798.

Nemeroff, C.B., Weinberger, D., Rutter, M., MacMillan, H.L., Bryant, R.A., Wessely, S., Stein, D.J., Pariante, C.M., Seemüller, F., Berk, M., Malhi, G.S., Preisig, M., Brüne, M., & Lysaker, P. (2013). DSM-5: A collection of psychiatrist views on the changes, controversies, and future directions. *BMC Medicine*, 11, 202.

Nicolò, G., Dimaggio, G., Popolo, R., Carcione, A., Procacci, M., Hamm, J., Buck, K.D., Pompili, E., Buccione, I., Lagrotteria, B., & Lysaker, P.H. (2012). Associations of metacognition with symptoms, insight and neurocognition in clinically stable outpatients with schizophrenia. *Journal of Nervous and Mental Disease*, 200(7), 644–647.

Nietzsche, F. (1886/1966). *Beyond good and evil.* Translated by W. Kaufman. New York: Random House.

Outcalt, J., Dimaggio, G., Popolo, R., Buck, K.D., Chaudoin-Patzoldt, K.A., George, S., Olesek, K.L., & Lysaker, P.H. (2016). Metacognition moderates the relationship of disturbances in attachment with severity of borderline personality disorder among persons in treatment for substance use disorders. *Comprehensive Psychiatry*, 64, 22–28.

Parnas, J. (2011). A disappearing heritage: The clinical core of schizophrenia. *Schizophrenia Bulletin*, 37, 1121–1130.

Parnas, J. & Handest, P. (2003). Phenomenology of anomalous self-experience in early schizophrenia. *Comprehensive Psychiatry*, 44, 121–134.

Phelan, J.C., Link, B.G., Stueve, A., & Pescosolido, B.A. (2000). Public conceptions of mental illness in 1950 and 1996: What is mental illness and is it to be feared? *Journal of Health and Social Behavior*, 41, 188–207.

Pinkham, A.E., Penn, D.L., Green, M.F., Buck, B., Healey, K., & Harvey, P.D. (2014). The social cognition psychometric evaluation study: Results of the expert survey and RAND panel. *Schizophrenia Bulletin*, 40(4), 813–823.

Popolo, R., Smith, E., Lysaker, P.H., Lesting, K., Cavallo, F., Melchiorre, L., Santone, C., & Dimaggio, G. (2017). Metacognitive profiles in schizophrenia and bipolar disorder: Comparisons with healthy controls and correlations with negative symptoms. *Psychiatry Research*, 257, 45–50.

Prouty G. (2003) Pre-therapy: A newer development in the psychotherapy of schizophrenia. *Journal of the Academy of Psychoanalysis and Dynamic Psychiatry*, 31(1), 59–73.

Ringer, J.M. & Lysaker, P.H. (2014). Anger expression styles in schizophrenia spectrum disorders: Associations with anxiety, paranoia, emotion recognition, and trauma history. *Journal of Nervous and Mental Disease*, 202(12), 853–858.

Roe, D. (2001). Exploring the relationship between the person and the disorder among individuals hospitalized for psychosis. *Psychiatry*, 62, 372–380.

Roe, D. (2005). Recovering from severe mental illness: Mutual influences of self and illness. *Journal of Psychosocial Nursing and Mental Health Services*, 43, 35–40.

Roe, D. & Ben-Yishai, A. (1999). Exploring the relationship between the person and the disorder among individuals hospitalized for psychosis. *Psychiatry: Interpersonal and Biological Processes*, 62, 370–380.

Roe, D. & Davidson, L. (2005). Self and narrative in schizophrenia: Time to author a new story. *Journal of Medical Humanities*, 31, 89–94.

Rosenbaum, B. (2005). Psychosis and the structure of homosexuality: Understanding the pathogenesis of schizophrenic states of mind. *Scandinavian Psychoanalytic Review*, 28, 82–89.

Sass, L.A. (2000). *Madness and modernism: Insanity in the light of modern art, literature, and thought.* Philadelphia, PA: John Benjamins Publishing Company.

Searles, H. (1965). *Collected papers of schizophrenia and related subjects.* New York: International Universities Press.

Seligman, M.E., Rashid, T., & Parks, A.C. (2006). Positive psychotherapy. *American Psychologist*, 61(8), 774–788.

Semerari, A., Carcione, A., Dimaggio, G., Falcone, M., Nicolò, G., Procacci, M., Alleva, G., & Mergenthaler, E. (2003). How to evaluate metacognitive function in psychotherapy? The metacognition assessment scale and its applications. *Clinical Psychology and Psychotherapy*, 10, 238–2861.

Semerari, A., Colle, L., Pellecchia, G., Buccione, I., Carcione, A., & Dimaggio, G., (2014). Metacognition: Severity and styles in personality disorders. *Journal of Personality Disorders*, 28(6), 751–766.

Silverstein, S.M. & Bellack, A.S. (2008). Scientific agenda for the concept of recovery as it applies to schizophrenia. *Clinical Psychology Review*, 28(7), 1108–1124.

Slade, M. (2009). *Personal recovery and mental illness: A guide for mental health professionals.* New York: Cambridge University Press.

Snethen, G., McCormick, B.P., & Lysaker, P.H. (2014). Physical activity and psychiatric symptoms in adults with schizophrenia spectrum disorders. *Journal of Nervous and Mental Disease*, 202(12), 845–852.

Stern, D.N. (2000). *The interpersonal world of the infant: A view from psychoanalysis and developmental psychology.* New York, NY: Basic Books.

Stout, R. (1983). *Fer-de-lance.* New York: Bantam Books.

Substance Abuse and Mental Health Services Administration. (2005). *National consensus conference on mental health recovery and systems transformation.* Rockville, MD: Department of Health and Human Services.

Sullivan, H.S. (1962). *Schizophrenia as a human process.* New York: Norton.

Tarricone, P. (2011). *The taxonomy of metacognition.* East Sussex: Psychology Press.

Tas, C., Brown, E.C., Aydemir, O., Brüne, M., & Lysaker, P.H. (2014). Metacognition in psychosis: Comparison of schizophrenia with bipolar disorder. *Psychiatry Research*, 219(3), 464–469.

Tas, C., Brown, E.C., Esen-Danaci, A., Lysaker, P.H., & Brüne, M. (2012). Intrinsic motivation and metacognition as predictors of learning potential in patients with remitted schizophrenia. *Journal of Psychiatric Research*, 46(8), 1086–1092.

Thompson, V.A., Prowse Turner, J.A., & Pennycook, G. (2011). Intuition, reason, and metacognition. *Cognitive Psychology*, 63(3), 107–140.

Torgalsboen, A. & Rund, B.R. (2002). Lessons learned from three studies of recovery from schizophrenia. *International Review of Psychiatry*, 14, 312–317.

Trauelsen, A.M., Gumley, A., Jansen, J.E., Pedersen, M.B., Nielsen, H.G., Trier, C.H., Haahr, U.H., & Simonsen, E. (2016). Metacognition in first-episode psychosis and its association with positive and negative symptom profiles. *Psychiatry Research*, 238, 14–23.

Velligan, D.I., Sajatovic, M., Hatch, A., Kramata, P., & Docherty, J.P. (2017). Why do psychiatric patients stop antipsychotic medication? A systematic review of reasons for nonadherence to medication in patients with serious mental illness. *Patient Preference and Adherence*, 11, 449–468.

Vlcek, P., Bob, P., & Raboch, J. (2014). Sensory disturbances, inhibitory deficits, and the P50 wave in schizophrenia. *Neuropsychiatric Disorders and Treatment*, 10, 1309–1315.

Vohs, J.L., George, S., Leonhardt, B.L., & Lysaker, P.H. (2016). An integrative model of the impairments in insight in schizophrenia: Emerging research on causal factors and treatments. *Expert Review of Neurotherapeutics*, 22, 1–12.

Vohs, J.L. & Leonhardt, B.L. (2016). Metacognitive reflection and insight therapy for borderline personality disorder: A case illustration of an individual in a long term institutional setting. *Journal of Contemporary Psychotherapy*, 46(4), 255–264.

Vohs, J.L., Leonhardt, B.L., James, A.V., Francis, M.M., Breier, A., Mehdiyoun, N., Visco, A.C., & Lysaker, P.H. (In press). Metacognitive Reflection and Insight Therapy for early psychosis: Effects on insight. *Schizophrenia Research.*

Vohs, J.L. & Lysaker, P.H. (2014). Metacognitive mastery and intrinsic motivation in schizophrenia. *Journal of Nervous and Mental Disease*, 202(1), 74–77.

Vohs, J.L., Lysaker, P.H., Francis, M., Hamm, J., Buck, K.D., Olesek, K., Outcalt, J., Dimaggio, G., Leonhardt, B., Liffick, E., Mehdiyoun, N., & Breier, A. (2014). Metacognition, social cognition, and symptoms in patients with first episode and prolonged psychosis. *Schizophrenia Research*, 153, 54–59.

WeiMing, W., Yi, D., Lysaker, P.H., & Kai, W. (2015a). The relationship among the metacognitive ability, empathy and psychotic symptoms in schizophrenic patients in a post-acute phase of illness. *Chinese Journal of Behavioral Medicine and Brain Science*, 24(2), 128–131.

WeiMing, W., Yi, D., Lysaker, P.H., Kai, W., Daomin, Z., Long, W., Yong, L., Yuting, M., Xuenquan, C., & Hui, L. (2015b). A correlation study of metacognition and theory of mind in the patients with schizophrenia. *Chinese Journal of Psychiatry*, 48(2), 98–104.

Wells, A. (2000). *Emotional disorders and metacognition: Innovative cognitive therapy.* New York, NY: John Wiley and Sons.

Will, O.A. (1967). Schizophrenia the problem of origins. In J. Romano (Ed.), *The origin of schizophrenia* (pp. 214–227). New York: Excerpta Medical Foundation.

Yanos, P.T., Roe, D., & Lysaker, P.H. (2010). The impact of illness identity on recovery from severe mental illness. *American Journal of Psychiatric Rehabilitation*, 13(2), 73–93.

Yanos, P.T., Roe, D., Markus, K., & Lysaker, P.H. (2008). Pathways between internalized stigma and outcomes related to recovery in schizophrenia-spectrum disorders. *Psychiatric Services*, 59, 1437–1442.

Index

adherence to treatment, measuring 135
agenda element of MERIT 44, 159; clarifying patients' agendas **46**, 46–48; clinical illustrations 50–52; complexity of 44–45; factors inhibiting detection of 48–50; importance of shared process 48; MERIT-TAS scale **52**; patient's uncertainty of 45–46, **46**
aggression, managing in patients 144–145
alcohol, comorbid substance abuse 141
ambassador of health stance 56–57
anger, managing in patients 144–145
anhedonia 69
antisocial behavior, managing in patients 144–145
arbiter of reality stance 55–56
assessing: awareness of the mind of the other 100–101, **114**, 114–118; decentration 103–104; mastery 101–103; metacognition 12–14, 25–27; *see also* MAS-A (Metacognition Assessment Scale-Abbreviated); self-reflectivity
assigning homework 139
authenticity, importance of 73–75
avoiding therapist demoralization 137–138
awareness of the mind of the other 18; assessing with O scale 100–101; O scale 157; stimulating **114**, 114–118

Bakhtin, M. 149–150
Bargenquast, R. 150
barriers to obtaining narrative episodes 65–66
basic assertions of MERIT 25
basic conditions for sharing therapist's thoughts 54–55
Beyond Good and Evil (Nietzsche, 1886) 150
Bleuler, Eugen 10–11; "Four A's" of schizophrenia 11
blood pressure analogy of metacognition 20
Borges, Jorge Luis 149
"broken brain" concept 3–4
burnout, avoiding 137–138

case studies on MERIT psychotherapy **151**, 151–152
challenges: of M interventions **127**; of O interventions 118; of S interventions 113; of severe mental illness 3–5
changes in patients' lives, querying about 86–88
clarifying patients' agendas **46**, 46–48
clinical illustrations for agenda element of MERIT 50–52, **52**
communication: explaining MERIT to patients 131–132; intersubjectivity 19–20; therapist's role as partner in dialogue 80–81
comorbid medical conditions 145
comorbid substance abuse 141
compassion fatigue, avoiding 137–138
complexity of patient's agenda 44–45
conceptual fragmentation: as cause of psychosis 11–12; *see also* integration
considerations when using MERIT-IF 104
content elements of MERIT: agenda 44–52, **52**; defining the

psychological problem 69–75; eliciting the narrative episode 61–67, **67**; insertion of the therapist's mind 53–57
crisis management 143

D scale **96**, 103–104, 158
decentration 18, **26**; assessing 103–104; D scale **96**, 158
deficits in metacognition, reasons for 21
defining the psychological problem element 69–76, **76**; common challenges in defining problems 71–73; evolution of psychological problems during treatment 75; inauthentic psychological problems 74–75; MERIT-TAS scale 75–76, **76**; threats to authenticity 73–75
dementia 10–11
dementia praecox 11
Dementia Praecox, or the Group of Schizophrenia (Jung, 1911) 10–11
demoralization, avoiding 137–138
detecting agendas of patients 48–50
Dewey, J., integration 17–18
dialogue: explaining MERIT to patients 131–132; interventions for sustaining **59**, 59–60; as meaning-making process 19–20; therapist's role as partner in 80–81; timing of discussions about progress 88
Dimaggio, Giancarlo 17–19
discrete processes of metacognition 17–18
disruptions in meaning-making process 9
The Divided Self (Laing, 1978) 149
drug abuse, comorbid substance abuse 141

early stage of MERIT 132–133
ego function in schizophrenia 23
elements of MERIT 7, **43**; defining the psychological problem element 69–76, **76**; eliciting the narrative episode 61–67, **67**; insertion of the therapist's mind 54–60, **60**; reflection on progress 85; stimulating mastery 121–127, **127**; stimulating reflections about the self and others **106**, 106–118; therapeutic relationship 79–83, **83**
eliciting the narrative episode 61–65; barriers to obtaining narrative episodes 65–66; MERIT-TAS scale **67**
emergence of psychological problems in sessions 70–71; common challenges in defining problems 71–73; evolution of psychological problems during treatment 75; "false" psychological problems 74–75
emotional intelligence 22
emotions: compassion fatigue, avoiding 137–138; and metacognition 6; O scale **94**; rage, managing in patients 144–145; and suicidality 141–142
entrenched illness identity 146
evolution of psychological problems during treatment 75
exacerbation of symptoms 142
experiences of therapists during sessions 135–137
explaining MERIT to patients 131–132
exploring narratives 62–65; barriers to obtaining narrative episodes 65–66

"false" psychological problems 74–75
fear: of being a pretender 138
Fer-de-Lance (Stout, 1983) 22
final stage of MERIT 133–134
focus of metacognition 18–19
fragmentation, S scale 92
Freud, Sigmund 11–12

group supervision approach to learning MERIT 135–137

history of trauma in patients, effect on therapeutic alliance 143–144
homework assignments 139
hospitalization of patients 143

illness-based identity 146
improvement in metacognition, impact on patient's emotional distress 38–40
inauthentic psychological problems 74–75
insertion of the therapist's mind element 53–54; basic conditions for sharing therapist's thoughts 54–55;

examples 53; MERIT-TAS scale 60; non-open stances 55–57; open stance 57–60; therapist's stance 55–57
integration: assessing metacognition 12–14; intersubjective nature of 19–20; mentalization 22; metacognition 17–18; S scale 92; synthetic-integrative functioning 23
intelligence, emotional intelligence 22
intersubjectivity: of metacognition 19–20; sharing thoughts 58–59
interventions 4, 6–7; awareness of the mind of the other, stimulating **106**, 106–112; characteristic interventions and outcomes for self-reflection **106**; elements 7; M interventions, common challenges in **127**; O interventions, common challenges in 118; S interventions, common challenges in 113; for stimulating mastery 121–126; for stimulating self-reflectivity **106**, 106–112; sustaining dialogue **59**, 59–60
introducing MERIT to patients 131–132
IPII (Indiana Psychiatric Illness Interview) **26**

Jung, Carl 10

"Kafka and His Precursors" 149
Kelly, George 150
Kesey, Ken 149
Kraepelin, Emil 11

Laing, R. D. 149
learning MERIT 135–137
length of MERIT treatment 134–135
literary influences on MERIT 149–150

M scale 92, **95**, 101–103, 158; mastery, stimulating 121–126
managing aggression in patients 144–145
MAS (Metacognition Assessment Scale) 25–26
MAS-A (Metacognition Assessment Scale-Abbreviated) 25–27; response of metacognition to treatment 28–29
mastery 18, **26**; common challenges in M interventions **127**; M scale 92, **95**, 101–103, 158; stimulating mastery element 121–127, **127**
meaning-making process: dialogue 19–20; disruptions in 9; improvement in metacognition, impact on patient's emotional distress 38–40
measuring: adherence to treatment 135; awareness of the mind of the other **114**, 114–118; mastery 121–126; metacognition 25
medication non-adherence, responding to 145–146
mental illness: challenges of 3–5; ego function in schizophrenia 23; "Four A's" of schizophrenia 11; initial symptoms of 9–10; metaphorical descriptions 3–4; pessimistic assumptions about 4; psychosis, Freud's description of 11–12; recovery from 4–5; stigma associated with 3; *see also* severe mental illness
mentalization 22
MERIT (Metacognitive Reflection and Insight Therapy) 5–6; active involvement of patients in their recovery as precondition 35–36; adherence to treatment 135; agenda element 44–52, **52**; basic assertions of 25; defining the psychological problem element 69–76, **76**; effect of increasing metacognitive capacity on emotional distress 38–40; elements **43**, 159–160; eliciting the narrative episode element 61–67, **67**; explaining to patients 131–132; insertion of the therapist's mind element 53–54; learning 135–137; length of treatment 134–135; literary influences on 149–150; metacognition 6, 17–18; open trials 150; phases of treatment 132–134; poor insight 145–146; possibility of recovery from severe mental illness as precondition 33–35; published case studies on MERIT psychotherapy **151**, 151–152; rate of change 134–135; reflection on progress element 85–89, **89**; social

stigma of mental illness, impact on patients 40; stimulating mastery element 121–127, **127**; termination of 134; therapeutic relationship element 79–83, **83**; therapist's role as consultant and equal participant as MERIT precondition 36–37; understandable nature of psychosis as precondition 37–38
MERIT Institute website 135–137
MERIT-IF (MERIT Intervention Framework) 29, 91–92; considerations when using 104; D scale **96**, 103–104, 158; M scale 92, **95**, 101–103, 158; metacognition, assessing **96**, 96–98; O scale 92, **94**, 100–101, 105, 157; rating form 161; S scale 92, **93**, 98–99, 105–112, 157; tracking scores 135
MERIT-TAS (MERIT-Therapist Adherence Scale): agenda element **52**; defining the psychological problem element 75–76, **76**; elements of MERIT 159–160; eliciting the narrative episode element **67**; insertion of the therapist's mind element **60**; rating form 161; reflection on progress element **89**; stimulating mastery element **127**; stimulating reflections about the self and others element 118–119, **119**; therapeutic relationship element **83**
metacognition 6, 9; assessing 12–14; blood pressure analogy of 20; as capacity 20–21; deficits in, reasons for 21; discrete processes of 17–18; and emotional intelligence 22; explaining to patients 131–132; focus of 18–19; improvement in, impact on emotional distress 38–40; as intersubjective act 19–20; intersubjectivity 19–20; MAS-A 25–27; mastery, stimulating 121–126; measuring disturbances in 25; and mentalization 22; MERIT-IF **96**, 96–98; MERIT's view of 17–18; and mindfulness 22; necessity of for survival 18–19; poor insight 145–146; as predictor of clinical outcomes 28–29; quality of life, effect on 28; social cognition 21–22
metaphorical descriptions of mental illness, "broken brain" concept 3–4
middle phase of MERIT 133
mindfulness 22
minister of comfort stance 57

narrative episodes 61; authenticity, importance of 73–75; barriers to obtaining 65–66; common challenges in defining problems 71–73; eliciting 62–65; eliciting the narrative episode element, MERIT-TAS scale **67**; emergence of psychological problems in sessions 70–71; *see also* eliciting the narrative episode element
necessity of metacognition for survival 18–19
negative experiences with previous mental health treatment, responding to 146–147
neural circuitry, disruptions in as cause of schizophrenia 12
Nietzsche, F. 18–19, 150
non-open stances: ambassador of health 56–57; arbiter of reality 55–56; minister of comfort 57; spokesperson 56

O scale 92, **94**, 100–101, 105, 157; awareness of the mind of the other, stimulating **114**, 114–118
objectivity, integrative process 14–15
One Flew Over the Cuckoo's Nest (Kesey, 1962) 149
open stances 57–60
open trials of MERIT 150

patients 7; as active agents in their recovery, MERIT precondition II 35–36; adherence to treatment, measuring 135; authenticity, importance of 73–75; barriers to obtaining narrative episodes 65–66; clarifying patients' agendas **46**, 46–48; common challenges in defining problems 71–73; complexity of agenda 44–52, **52**; detecting agendas 48–50; emergence of psychological

problems in sessions 70–71; evolution of psychological problems during treatment 75; exacerbation of symptoms 142; history of trauma, effect on therapeutic alliance 143–144; homework assignments 139; hospitalization of 143; impact of therapist's role on patient 81–82; MERIT, explaining 131–132; narrative episodes, eliciting 62–65; negative experiences with previous mental health treatment 146–147; querying about change 86–88; rate of change during MERIT treatment 134–135; reaction to therapist's role 82; shared process, importance of 48, 58–59; social stigma of mental illness, impact on 40; suicidality 141–142; sustaining dialogue with **59**, 59–60; therapist conformance with patient positioning 82; uncertainty of agenda 45–46, **46**
persecutory delusions 38
pessimistic assumptions about mental illness 4
pharmacotherapy 4; medication non-adherence, responding to 145–146
phases of MERIT 132–134
poor insight 145–146
preconditions for MERIT **41**; increasing metacognitive capacity, effect on emotional distress 38–40; patient's active involvement in their recovery 35–36; recovery from severe mental illness is possible 33–35; social stigma of mental illness, impact on patients 40; therapist's role as consultant and equal participant 36–37; understandable nature of psychosis 37–38
prerequisites for recovery 147
pretending, fear of 138
pre-therapy 107
Problems of Dostoyevsky's Poetics (Bakhtin, 1929/1984) 149–150
process elements of MERIT **43**; reflection on progress 85–89, **89**; reflection on therapeutic relationship 79–83, **83**
progress, reflecting on: asking about progress 85–86; querying about change 86–88; timing of discussions about progress 88
psychic pain 96–97
psychoanalysis: ego function in schizophrenia 23; mentalization 22
psychological problems, emergence of in sessions 70–71
psychological trauma, impact on metacognition 21
psychosis: active involvement of patients in their recovery from as MERIT precondition 35–36; defining the psychological problem element 70; entrenched illness identity 146; evolution of psychological problems during treatment 75; exacerbation of symptoms 142; Freud's description of 11–12; medication non-adherence, responding to 145–146; possibility of recovery from as MERIT precondition 33–35; stimulating self-reflectivity **106**, 106–112; understandable nature of as MERIT precondition 37–38
psychotherapy 5–6, 8; fear of being a pretender 138; patients 7; phases of MERIT 132–134; published case studies on MERIT psychotherapy **151**, 151–152
published case studies on MERIT psychotherapy **151**, 151–152
purpose of MERIT, explaining to patients 132

quality of life, effect of impaired metacognition on 28
quantifying metacognition 25–27
querying about change 86–88

rage, managing in patients 144–145
rate of change in patients during MERIT treatment 134–135
rating form for MERIT-IF 161
recovery from mental illness 4–5
recovery from severe mental illness: active involvement of patients as MERIT precondition 35–36; possibility of as MERIT precondition 33–35; prerequisites for 147
reflection on progress element 85; asking about progress 85–86;

MERIT-TAS scale **89**; querying about change 86–88; synergy with other elements 88–89, **89**; timing of discussions about progress 88
research studies on MERIT 150–153
responding to threats of aggression 144–145
response of metacognition to treatment 28–29

S scale 92, **93**, 105, 157; assessing self-reflectivity with 98–99; characteristic interventions and outcomes for self-reflection **106**; measuring impairments in self-reflection **106**, 106–112
schizophrenia 3; *Collected Papers on Schizophrenia and Related Subjects* (Searle, 1965) 149; conceptual fragmentation 11–12; defining the psychological problem element 70; ego function in 23; entrenched illness identity 146; "Four A's" of 11; MAS-A 25–27; medication non-adherence, responding to 145–146; neural circuitry, disruptions in as cause of 12; "self" of persons with 10; stigma associated with 7; stimulating self-reflectivity **106**, 106–112; threats of violence, responding to 144–145; understandable nature of psychosis as MERIT precondition 37–38; *see also* psychosis
schizophrenia spectrum disorders 7–8
Schweitzer, R.D.
Searle, Harold 149
"self," of schizophrenics 10
self-disclosure 138–139
self-reflectivity 18, **26**; assessing with S scale 98–99; characteristic interventions and outcomes **106**; measuring **106**, 106–112; S scale 92, **93**, 157; *see also* metacognition; S scale
Semerari, Antonio 17–19; MAS 25–25, **26**
severe mental illness: challenges of 3–5; ego function in schizophrenia 23; exacerbation of symptoms 142; "Four A's" of schizophrenia 11; initial symptoms of 9–10; pessimistic assumptions about 4; possibility of recovery from as MERIT precondition 33–35; psychosis, Freud's description of 11–12; recovery from 4–5
shared process, importance of 48, 58–59; interventions for sustaining dialogue **59**, 59–60
social cognition 21–22
spokesperson stance 56
stances of therapists: ambassador of health stance 56–57; arbiter of reality stance 55–56; minister of comfort stance 57; non-open stance 55–57; spokesperson stance 56
stigma associated with mental illness 3, 7; impact on patients 40; schizophrenia 7
stimulating: awareness of the mind of the other **114**, 114–118; mastery 121–126; self-reflectivity **106**, 106–112
substance abuse 141
suicidality 141–142
superordinate elements of MERIT **43**
supervision approach to learning MERIT 135–137
survival, necessity of metacognition for 18–19
sustaining dialogue **59**, 59–60
symptoms, exacerbation of 142
synthetic-integrative functioning 23

Tarricone, P. 17
termination of MERIT 134
terminology used in this book 7–8
therapeutic relationship element 79; components of 79–80; impact of therapist's role on patient 81–82; MERIT-TAS scale **83**; perceptions of therapist's role as partner in dialogue 80–81; therapist conformance with patient positioning 82
therapists: ambassador of health stance 56–57; arbiter of reality stance 55–56; barriers to obtaining narrative episodes 65–66; clarifying patients' agendas **46,** 46–48; crisis management 143; demoralization, avoiding 137–138; experiences of during therapy sessions

135–137; explaining MERIT to patients 131–132; fear of being a pretender 138; insertion of the therapist's mind element 53–54; learning MERIT 135–137; mastery, stimulating 121–126; narrative episodes, eliciting 62–65; open stances 57–60; querying about change 86–88; role as consultant and equal participant as MERIT precondition 36–37; self-disclosure 138–139; shared process, importance of 48, 58–59; spokesperson stance 56; sustaining dialogue **59**, 59–60; timing of discussions about progress 88
therapy: adherence to treatment, measuring 135; assigning homework 139; common challenges in defining problems 71–73; emergence of psychological problems in sessions 70–71; evolution of psychological problems 75; medication non-adherence, responding to 145–146; MERIT 5–6; negative experiences with previous mental health treatment, responding to 146–147; open trials of MERIT 150; phases of MERIT 132–134; pre-therapy 107; psychic pain 96–97; published case studies on MERIT psychotherapy **151**, 151–152; rate of change in patients during MERIT treatment 134–135; response of metacognition to treatment 28–29; termination of MERIT 134
thought: basic conditions for sharing therapist's thoughts 54–55; insertion of the therapist's mind element 53–54; intersubjectivity 19–20
threats of violence, responding to 144–145
threats to authenticity 73–75
timing of discussions about progress 88
tracking MERIT-IF scores 135
training opportunities for MERIT 135–137
trauma: history of in patients, effect on therapeutic alliance 143–144; impact on metacognition 21

uncertainty of patient's agenda 45–46, **46**
understandable nature of psychosis as MERIT precondition 37–38
understanding other's minds **26**; O scale 92, **94**; *see also* O scale

variability in metacognition 20–21

websites, MERIT Institute 135–137